CW01085125

LITTLE CHEVERELL

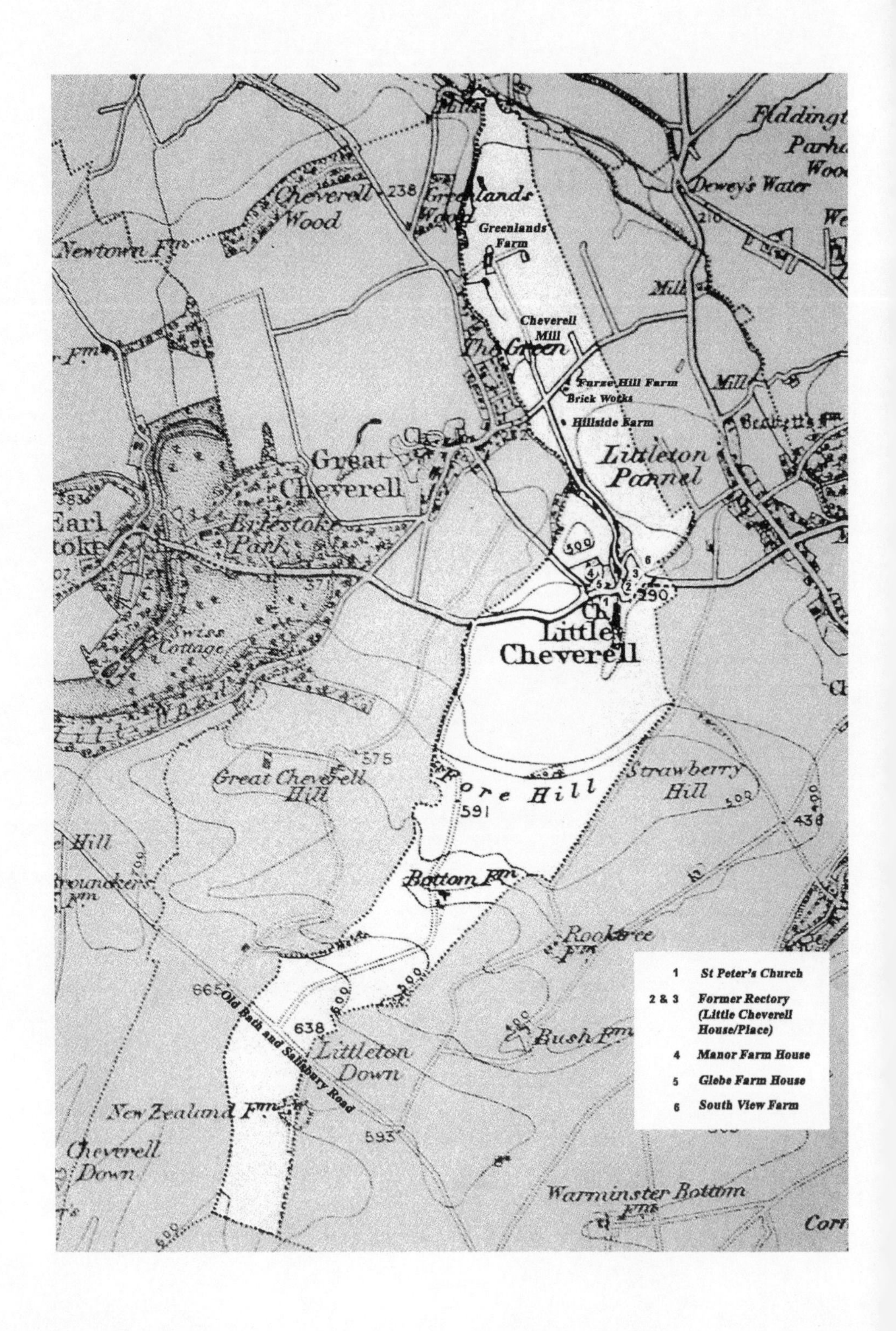

Cheverell Wood
238
Greenlands Wood
Greenlands Farm
Newtown Fm
Dewey's Water
Mill
Cheverell Mill
The Green
Furze Hill Farm
Brick Works
Hillside Farm
Mill
Littleton Pannel
Great Cheverell
Erlestoke Park
300
290
Little Cheverell
Swiss Cottage
575
Great Cheverell Hill
Fore Hill
591
Strawberry Hill
436
Bottom Fm
Rooktree Fm
665
Old Bath and Salisbury Road
638
Littleton Down
Bush Fm
New Zealand Fm
593
Cheverell Down
Warminster Bottom Fm
1 St Peter's Church
2 & 3 Former Rectory (Little Cheverell House/Place)
4 Manor Farm House
5 Glebe Farm House
6 South View Farm

LITTLE CHEVERELL

The History of a Wiltshire Village

DONALD HAWLEY

MICHAEL RUSSELL

DEDICATED TO THE LATE

MARGARET NURSE

IN RECOGNITION OF HER LOVE

OF THE VILLAGE

AND GENEROUS LEGACY FOR

LITTLE CHEVERELL

© Donald Hawley 2007

The right of Sir Donald Hawley to be identified
as the author of this work has been asserted by him
in accordance with the Copyright, Designs
and Patents Act, 1988

First published in Great Britain 2007
by Michael Russell (Publishing) Ltd
Wilby Hall, Wilby, Norwich NR16 2JP

Page makeup in Sabon by Waveney Typesetters
Wymondham, Norfolk
Printed and bound in Great Britain
by Biddles Ltd, King's Lynn, Norfolk

All rights reserved
ISBN 978-0-85955-310-0

Contents

Foreword

I have many acknowledgements to make for help received in the production of this book. For the personal accounts of life in the village I am most grateful for the generous assistance of all the people I approached. Ken and Greta Taylor in particular proved mines of information and Mike Brain, who coordinated the photographs from his own rich collection, also read the whole manuscript and made very helpful suggestions. Helena Warnock kindly transcribed a number of accounts of their recollections written by members of the village.

Most of the photographs, apart from those taken by Mike Brain himself, were shown at an exhibition in the village for the Millennium and gratitude is due to all who have made them available. In making a selection of these, and of other material, I have tried to illustrate the various aspects of village life, but it has not been possible of course to use all the material. I hope this may not give rise to disappointment on anyone's part.

I would also like to thank John d'Arcy, County Archivist, and the Wiltshire County Record Office in Trowbridge for permission to photograph the 1722 map and include it in the book, as well as for all the help they gave me. Likewise I am indebted to John Chandler for his kind permission to use part of the map of local parishes on page vi of his book *Devizes and Central Wiltshire*. Credit for photographing the 1722 map goes to Mike Brain and Bill Palmer, who also kindly spent a considerable amount of time finalising the maps for publication. The painting of the church is reproduced by kind permission of the Devizes Museum.

I owe much as well to Bryan Coupe, Jim Hodges and Lorna Haycock for contributing their local knowledge and drawing my attention to important sources which I would otherwise have missed, as well as reading the manuscript and making very valuable suggestions. I have to thank Joanna Buckley too for reading the proofs so carefully and for making numerous detailed proposals. Throughout I have had great support and encouragement from my wife Ruth and I thank her for all this and, far from least, partnership in producing the index.

Little Cheverell, August 2007 DONALD HAWLEY

The Village

Already featuring in the Domesday Book, Little Cheverell dates back at least to Saxon times and remains as small a village as it has always been.

ORIGIN OF NAME

To the Roman poet Vergil 'capreolus' meant a roebuck or chamois, as the French 'chevreuil' still does. Norman documents in the early twelfth century termed the village Capreolum,[1] though the – earlier – Domesday Survey of 1086 already called it 'Chevrel'. Roebuck – much prized in the past for the excitement of the chase and for venison – still run nearby and this would explain the origin of the name. An amalgamation, however, of Middle Welsh 'kyuar' meaning ploughland and ancient British 'ial' meaning fertile upland does describe the geographical situation precisely and is, according to some, the real origin of 'Cheverell'. There are also those who would attribute the name to 'Chervil' – an Old English word for a pot-herb (*anthriscus cerefolium*) with aromatic leaves used to flavour soups, although the logic of this is less easy to follow.

There is yet another possibility. 'Cheverel' or 'cheveril', according to the *Oxford English Dictionary*, means a kid and is derived from 'chevrelle', an old French diminutive of 'chèvre' (Latin *capra*). First quoted in sixteenth- and seventeenth-century literature, it referred to kid leather and came to mean flexible, stretchable or elastic and to 'cheverelize' was 'to stretch a point'. Stubbes wrote of lawyers' 'chauerell consciences', whilst in Shakespeare's *Romeo and Juliet* Mercutio teases Romeo: 'Oh, here's a wit of cheveril, that stretches from an inch narrow to an ell broad'; and in *King Henry VIII* an old lady of the court urges Anne Boleyn, who was then still lady in waiting to Queen Catherine, to stretch her 'soft cheveril conscience' to please

1 Lewis and Short, *A Latin Dictionary*.

the king. At first sight this might seem the most obvious explanation of the name but, on the other hand, the use of 'cheverel' in this sense seems to date only from a period long after the name of the village is known to have been in existence.

THE PARISH

Viewed from the air the parishes surrounding the north and west of Salisbury Plain[2] resemble, in their long thin shapes, the tentacles of an octopus and they took their form from the mixed farming needs of Saxon manors.[3] The parish[4] of Little Cheverell (Cheverell Parva) was therefore constituted from before the Norman Conquest as a strip four miles long, though less than a mile wide at any point, consisting of a settlement in the vale with clay soils for tilling; meadow and pasture on upper greensand nearby; and pasture on the chalk uplands accessed by drove roads leading to the scarp of Cheverell Cliff, Forehill and Salisbury Plain. It stretches from the parish of Imber in the south to Worton in the north and the other neighbouring parishes are Great Cheverell to the west – separated in part from the village by the Hawkswell stream – and West Lavington with Littleton Panell to the east. Some of the inhabited part of the village itself grew up around the church and manor and another part along the line of the Hawkswell stream, which is joined by a small tributary.

THE VILLAGERS

The village has no known poet such as Thomas Gray and it is not easy to conjure up a vision of people's lives in former times when few were endowed with abundant earthly goods; few owned books or much furniture; a bequest of clothes was not insignificant and educational opportunities were limited. Parts of Thomas Gray's famous elegy written in the churchyard of Stoke Poges might, however, almost as well have been inspired one evening in the churchyard of Little Cheverell:

2 The parishes on the northern side of the Vale of Pewsey also tend to have similar long thin shapes.

3 Andrew Reynolds, *Later Anglo-Saxon England*, Tempus Publishing Ltd, 1999, pp. 82–4.

4 The ecclesiastical and civil parishes have always been identical.

> The curfew tolls the knell of passing day,
> The lowing herd winds slowly o'er the lea,
> The ploughman homeward plods his weary way…
>
> Beneath those rugged elms,[5] that yew-tree's shade,
> Where heaves the turf in many a mouldering heap,
> Each in his narrow cell for ever laid,
> The rude Forefathers[6] of the hamlet sleep…
>
> Oft did the harvest to their sickle yield,
> Their furrow oft the stubborn glebe has broke;…
>
> But Knowledge to their eyes her ample page
> Rich with the spoils of time did ne'er unroll;
> Chill Penury repressed their noble rage,
> And froze the genial current of the soul….
>
> Along the cool sequestered vale of life
> They kept the noiseless tenor of their way.

It is a little tantalising that William Cobbett, on his 'Rural Ride' on horseback from Salisbury to Highworth in 1826, did not pass through the village, for we might have had his eyewitness impressions had he not ridden direct to Devizes from Erlestoke, which he did describe. It agreeably impressed him:

> Every house is white and the front of every one is covered with some sort or other of clematis, or with rose-trees, or jasmines. It was easy to guess that the whole village belonged to one owner; and that owner I found to be a Mr Watson Taylor, whose very pretty seat is close by the hamlet, and in whose park I saw what I never saw before, namely some black swans.

Although William Cobbett was a prominent reformer, politician and author who championed traditional rural England against the changes brought about by the Industrial Revolution, he was also the son of a farmer and innkeeper and started life himself as a crow scarer. This background created in him a down-to-earth humanity and common

5 Elms were a feature of Little Cheverell churchyard until the advent of Dutch elm disease in the 1970s.

6 Gray was not being offensive or condescending. Note that he gave the forefathers a capital 'F' and 'rude' in his day meant 'simple or uncomplicated'.

sense, which enabled him to recognise that popular unrest in the countryside was mainly caused by unemployment and hunger. What he wrote about this part of the country is therefore of particular interest and illustrates something of general conditions prevailing at that particular time.

At Heytesbury, for instance, where he met a group of six young men and two boys, he witnessed serious poverty and heard at first hand how people's lives were affected by the rapid decline of the rural cloth industry. The young men were so 'extremely ragged' that Cobbett was moved to forgo both dinner and breakfast and, instead, to give them a square meal – two quartern loaves, two pounds of cheese and eight pints of strong beer. The landlord of the inn where he stayed was so affected by this act of compassion that he did not present his bill for the night, although Cobbett eventually persuaded him to take his due.

It was a search for nuts which had taken the members of this group to Heytesbury and gave Cobbett the chance to hear their story. They had been employed at broadcloth weaving in the factories of Bradford-on-Avon and, as recently as nine months before, had had full-time piecework at one shilling and threepence a yard. This had been the rate paid 'at all times within the memory of man' but, despite this, their wage had been reduced to one shilling a yard with only quarter-time work. Although the reduction of wages had caused a 'turn out', the demonstration of protest had, Cobbett noted, been 'put an end to in the usual way; the constable's staff, the bayonet, the gaol'.

The difference between Cobbett's impressions of the local towns of Westbury and Warminster was very wide. Westbury was a 'nasty, odious, rotten borough'[7] of great ancient grandeur, which had once been ten or twenty times its then size. It had been affected by the quick decline of the cloth industry and both houses and factories had become run down. Warminster on the other hand he found a 'really nice and good town' and – perhaps something of a gourmet – he greatly admired the quality of the lamb and veal.

The decline of the rural broadcloth industry on which Cobbett commented so trenchantly must also have had its effect in villages such as Little Cheverell. The inhabitants, however, may have been sheltered from abject poverty by their other, mainly agricultural, activities. Cobbett's description of the agricultural scene was rosier. As he passed

7 'Rotten boroughs' were shortly to be abolished by the Reform Act of 1832.

Bratton, Edington and Erlestoke, he remarked that the turnips were very good for several miles and that the land was singularly fine and rich. It was September and he found the orchards 'very fine, finely sheltered, and the crops of apples and pears and walnuts very abundant'. Walnuts were 'a month earlier than usual'.

The road, the B3098, which he took from Westbury to Devizes ran along the 'line of separation between what they call South Wilts and North Wilts'. The former – on the right of his route – consisted of 'high and broad downs and narrow valleys with meadows and rivers running down them' and the latter of 'rather flat enclosed country'. The country on his right 'having a chalk bottom was for lean sheep and corn' and that on his left 'on marl, clay or flat stone was for cattle, fat sheep, cheese and bacon'. In commenting on this classical Wiltshire division between 'chalk and cheese', Cobbett found the chalk 'by far the most beautiful'. The people of Little Cheverell have the choice of deciding which part of their parish, which combines chalk and cheese, possesses more virtues.

The villagers who kept the 'noiseless tenor of their way' in earlier times included farmers, labourers, millers, brickmakers, hurdle makers, wheelwrights, gardeners, woodmen, grocers, shopkeepers, coal merchants, licensed beer sellers, weavers, spinners and even latterly a bicycle maker. A number, listed as gardeners in the records, grew food for the local market. An account of the village in the second half of the nineteenth century[8] – when many rural skills now lost were still practised – describes the farm workers as 'honest and high principled, happy and contented in spite of low wages'.[9] Families benefited from the work done in the fields at harvest time by the women. Wearing their bonnets and sack aprons, they earned a shilling a day as wages. The ancient custom which allowed gleaning between the corn stooks was also a considerable help to poor families and it was long a common

8 'Little Cheverell – As it was Sixty to a Hundred Years Ago'. Typed manuscript – undated and unsigned but apparently written around 1950 – in the possession of the author.

9 'Little Cheverell Village History' – an undated compilation made in typed manuscript form with photographs, believed to have been made in the 1950s by the ladies of the Women's Institute. Those who helped compile it were: Miss Helen Awdry, Mrs Olive Awdry, Mrs Beaven, Mrs Cowley, Mrs Draper, Miss Holloway, Mrs Hoffmann, Miss Lye and Mrs Reynolds.

sight to see a woman walking home through the village – her children running along beside her – with gleaned corn stalks on her head.

THE CURFEW

Whether the curfew[10] was tolled in Little Cheverell as it was in Stoke Poges cannot be established with certainty, though it probably was. Certainly the custom was still followed until relatively recent times in many parts of England[11] and it was also customary practice in parishes round the Salisbury Plain for sextons to toll the church bells to guide travellers on their way when mist and fog descended.

NAMES

A number of family names were constant in the village over many centuries and the name of Bolter is one of the earliest found. Christopher Bolter appears in a manorial rent book of 1582 as a tenant of two parcels of land with common grazing rights. Parish records are only available from the seventeenth century onwards but they and the gravestones in the churchyard show the continuity of a number of names. Among these are: Axford (1711);[12] Beaven [Biffin] (1797); Bolter (1622); Boulter (1657); Butcher (1720) Comelyn [Cumlyn] (1658); Crouch (1741); Edwards (1670); Hayward (1626); Hiscock (1675); Ladd (1728); Long (1628); Oram (1764); Maggs (1802); Minety [or Minty] (1701); Nightingal (1769); Phillips (1701); Ridout (1805); Sainsbury (1710); Smith (1656); Webb [also spelt Weabe] (1622); Weekes (1667); Wilkins (1700).[13] In earlier court records other names like de Aune (Anne), Norton, Russell, Stampford, Townsend, and Wadman appear.

Almost all of these surnames have now disappeared from the village

10 Curfew derives from the French 'couvre feu' and the custom of ringing the curfew bell was practised throughout Europe from before the Norman period – essentially as a fire precaution reminding people that it was time to cover their fires and go to bed. It was imposed in England as a security measure by William I, although strict observance was abolished by Henry I in 1100.

11 The curfew bell is still rung daily at Winchester Cathedral.

12 The dates given are the earliest discovered in the Parish records, but names may well be considerably older than the date given.

13 There may well be earlier entries of other once common names in various other records.

itself, even though they are still found in nearby places. Bill Phillips and Peter Edwards and his mother Sheila, however, are among those still living in Little Cheverell, whose family names have been known in the village for 300 years or more. The once prominent and common names of Bolter (and Boulter) and Axford on the other hand are no more.

A number of curious or recondite surnames appear in the records including: Cocket, Daudett, Flux, Kill, Paradiso, Planke, Purchase, Skull, Spire and Tinker. Rarer Christian names appearing include: Abigail, Abithel, Damaris, Dionysia, ffrizia, Genneverah, Gretian, Meliora, Prospera, Ursulie, and Shusannah.

Parish records also shed some light on contemporary life and social and religious attitudes, particularly in the seventeenth and eighteenth centuries. For instance an entry for Hugh Boulter in 1665 reveals that he 'was killed in a well the 30th October at Market Lavington'. In the same year 'Elizabeth a bastard child of Elizabeth Newmans' was buried. In 1790 'Richard baseborn son of Sarah Howell' was buried. In 1763 'William son of Eliz. Coles (base born)' was baptised and in 1773 another boy was baptised 'William son of Matthew Somner of Gt. Cheverell spuriously begot on the body of Elizabeth Wicks of this parish'. In 1759 Francis Bird, 'a vagrant beggar', was buried.

POPULATION

The inhabitants of Little Cheverell have never been numerous – appreciably less than the average village in the area – and it is known that in 1377 there were only 56 poll tax payers, compared with 73 in Great Cheverell. It was, however, not until 1785 that the earliest recorded comprehensive census was carried out. It was done by the then Rector, the Revd William Richards, who divided the parish into three divisions: the first in the neighbourhood of the church and the demesne farm, consisting of 16 houses and 69 people; the second, from the Rectory to half way down the valley, consisting of 15 houses and 72 people; and the third, which embraced Cheverell Mill, Greenlands Farm and cottages in the north of the valley to the west of Fuzzy's Hill, with 12 houses and 42 people.

The grand total was, therefore, 43 houses and 183 people, of whom 22 had the name of Bolter (or Boulter) – though by 1851 people of this name numbered 56, no less than 22% of the village. The general population fluctuated but, in the nineteenth century, rose to 263 in 1821 and to 295 (131 males and 164 females) in 1841, after which it declined to 255 by 1851 and to 234 (118 males and 116 females) by 1871. The decline in the female population was attributed principally to the young women going out to service,[14] but periodic agricultural depression in the nineteenth century and the demand for farm hands declining in the twentieth century as a result of mechanisation led to more general emigration from the village. By the 1940s the population had shrunk to about 150; in 1971 it was 155 and in 2000 141.

VILLAGE HOUSES

The houses, which stretched for many centuries along Low Road, were built by the lord of the manor largely for agricultural workers. Those standing today are not much older than the eighteenth or nineteenth centuries but, bearing such lovely names as Rose Cottage, Myrtle Cottage, Yew Tree Cottage, Holly Cottage, Fir Tree Cottage and Beech Cottage, still retain something of their older character despite modernisation.

Very few houses have been added to the village in the last fifty years, although a few have been demolished. Two bungalows, Fairwater and Edith's Marsh,[15] were privately built by Ridouts the builders at the north east end of Low Road in the 1960s and further south Coldharbour[16] and Cedar Croft[17] were also privately built in 1966.

Orchard Acre, where Vincent and Pam Gaiger now live, was built in bungalow style by Harry Smith the builder for Mr and Mrs Pike (she the sister of John Wilfred Nosworthy). Ashley was built in what was originally part of the garden by David Cooper when he acquired Beech Cottage from Ben Bolter in the 1960s.

The last two semi-detached cottages in the village on the road to Westbury, numbers 999 and 1000, are known as Piggery Cottages, as they were built close to earlier pig styes, and for long were occupied by those working on Manor Farm. They were built in about 1915 by W. Hopkins and Son of Market Lavington, probably for the Awdry family

14 Answers given by the rector to a series of formal inquiries in 1862 (1862 Inquiry). Document held in the library of Devizes Museum.
15 Formerly known as Brookside.
16 By Mike Brain personally.
17 Jack and Eve Wood built it for themselves.

when they held the manor. Before the Second World War four more houses were built a little further east along the B3098 by the local Council and, after the war, a further four were added. The Council sold all of these to the Sarsen Housing Association in the 1980s, although some have subsequently been bought outright. The four houses between the B3098 and Manor Farm were originally built in the 1960s by the War Department. West House, The Chimes and the bungalow adjacent to them were built in 1980[18] on the site of a number of redundant farm buildings and cottages opposite the church pulled down in the 1970s. In the 1980s Alan Harley built a new house on the south side of the B3098.

Details are given elsewhere about Hawkswell House, the Rectory (later Little Cheverell House and Cheverell Place), Manor House Farm, and East Sands and their occupants. Hawkswell Lodge dates from the creation of the modern Hawkswell estate between 1914 and 1920 and was lived in by James Fitch, Colonel Robert Awdry's coachman, whose life spanned an era when horse transport rapidly gave way to the motor car. He lived there until 1947, after which WD workers – including Bob Allard – occupied the house until it became the property of Michael and Judy Gaiger who considerably extended it.

The village has changed radically in the last fifty or so years but people still alive today clearly remember the names and occupations of all the families, and the houses they lived in, during the 1930s and 1940s when dependence on local agriculture directly or indirectly was still complete. These recollections depict a picture of a close-knit rural community with just a few depending on employment in Devizes or closer at hand (Appendix A).

NEOLITHIC, BRONZE AND IRON AGES

Some early settlement in the northern part of the village is suggested by a small find of flint tools and arrows from various periods long preceding the Roman occupation. In the Neolithic period – 3710 to 2000 BC – when Avebury and Stonehenge were built, Salisbury Plain is believed to have been thickly wooded with oak and yew, while the people tended

18 Owned respectively now by Wing Commander Victor and Margaret King and David Vernon Jones. The bungalow has had several owners but in 2006 it was acquired by Mr and Mrs Heather.

to establish their settlements near streams and rivers – with animal pens for sheep, goats, cattle and pigs. This practice confirms the real possibility that there was some early occupation along the line of the Hawkswell stream and, since the village lies within the so-called 'Wessex Triangle' of Avebury, Winchester and Warminster,[19] any people living where Little Cheverell now is may have participated in the great cultural and religious festivals at Avebury and Stonehenge.

Less speculative are the visible earthworks of the hill forts established nearby in the later Bronze and the subsequent Iron Age – approximately 1000 BC until the Roman occupation. Traces of ancient fields and numerous trees and bushes still mark the routes of old roads and tracks. The antiquarian Sir Richard Colt Hoare wrote:[20]

> A British village ... is situated on a piece of down called Little Cheverell, and in a direction towards the old road or track from Bath to Salisbury. It occupies the declivities of two hills, which terminate in a vale leading towards Imber and produces all the marks of an extensive British village, the entrance into which, between two slight banks, is very evident. It is truly interesting to trace with certainty the early residences of our ancestors and to find them so unexpectedly amidst the dreary regions of our extensive downs ... [and to find that] a district ... now the most defective in modern cultivation proves the most abundant in ancient population.

THE ROMAN PERIOD

When the Romans came, they stamped their culture and administration on the indigenous British people between 55 BC and the final withdrawal of the Roman legions in AD 414; and judging by Roman coins and second to fourth century pottery found in or near the village, Roman or Romano-British influence was strong in the immediate area. The whole immediate area was perhaps occupied by, or under the sway of, the Celtic Atrebates tribe – one of the major late Iron Age tribes in southern Britain. Their centre at Calleva Atrebatum

19 *Prehistoric Sacred Sites of Wessex*, Wessex Books.
20 *The Ancient History of Wiltshire*, vol. I, 1812, p. 95. Republished in 1975 by EP Publishing Ltd in collaboration with Wiltshire County Library.

– the modern Silchester some seven miles to the south west of Reading – probably lay within in the semi-autonomous 'client kingdom' of Cogibdunus,[21] and later became one of the main cities of Roman Britain. Little Cheverell village might, however, conceivably have fallen more within the influence of a more southerly tribe, the Durotriges, who were renowned as doughty defenders of their hill forts – although their main area of dominance was to the south and west. The truth is not easy to find.

ALFRED AND THE DANES

After the sunset of the Roman empire, lack of written records makes the period which witnessed invasions by Angles, Saxons and, later, Danes an obscure one. However the area was certainly occupied by the West Saxons, as shown by evidence of a Saxon settlement built on a former Roman site at Market Lavington. By the ninth century it was part of the Kingdom of Wessex under King Alfred and in AD 878 an event of great importance in English history, which must have affected Little Cheverell, probably took place only about four miles away. This was the Battle of Ethendune at Edington,[22] at which Alfred and his troops defeated a Danish force under Guthrum, their king. It is not impossible that some men from the village were among those summoned to the 'Fyrd'[23] to which Alfred called the Thanes and able-bodied freemen of Wiltshire along with those of Somerset and Hampshire in preparation for the battle.

The Anglo Saxon Chronicle recorded the event:

> In the 7th week after Easter, he (Alfred) rode to Brixton by the eastern side of Selwood and there came out to meet him all the people of Somerset and Wiltshire and that part of Hampshire

21 Literature published by the Department of Archaeology at Reading University on the Silchester site 2002.

22 Not all historians agree that Ethendune, the scene of the battle, was Edington but the preferred opinion seems to be that it was.

23 The obligation to contribute to the fyrd as the military force of the country was one element of the 'trinoda necessitas' imposed in Saxon times on all who possessed land including the Church , the others being bryge-bot – the obligation to maintain bridges and highways – and burg-bote – the obligation to maintain fortresses in an efficient state of defence.

> which is this side the sea and within one nyght after he proceeded to Heddington [*sic* – for Edington] and there fought with all the army and put them to flight.

Chippenham had previously fallen to Guthrum, who probably approached Ethendune from there, and it was to Chippenham that Alfred chased him back. There Guthrum surrendered and Alfred who, combining learning and Christian piety with notable success as a military commander, converted him to Christianity and personally baptised him. Thereupon Alfred, in a statesmanlike move, recognised him as king of his existing dominions and by this action of reconciliation changed the course of history, opening the way to the major changes in English law, education, religion and life itself which he inspired. Despite these successes the village may not have been totally immune from the further later Danish raids into Wiltshire, which took place in the first fifteen years of the eleventh century.

THE NORMAN LEGACY

Just as the Romans impressed their culture and administration on England, so did another continental power in the eleventh century – the Normans. William the Conqueror's defeat of King Harold at the Battle of Hastings in 1066 had very profound effects on government, land tenure, the administration of justice and life generally throughout the country; and Little Cheverell was not exempt. The Norman takeover from the Saxons was complete and their castle at Devizes only six miles away, probably first built between 1086 and 1099, was a constant reminder of their supremacy. One method by which this was demonstrated was the imposition of Norman feudal landholding. William's victory was regarded as having legitimated his claim to be King of England as true heir of King Edward the Confessor and consequently ultimate owner of all the land in the country. Some former English landholders, who submitted to him, were able to redeem their possessions but the greater part of the land, owned by the many who opposed him, was forfeited and granted to William's Norman followers, who thus became 'tenants' of the King. Although a strong system of justice and method of maintaining the King's Peace was gradually to emerge and shape national history, it was a grim time for the former Saxon leaders.

It seems that the lord of the Saxon manor of Little Cheverell was among those directly affected and dispossessed, for the Domesday Book of 1086 – the massive land survey commissioned by William I – records (English translation):

> Lethelin holds [Little] Cheverell of Ernulf. Aelward held it TRE [Tempus Regis Edwardi; in the time of Edward the Confessor], and it paid geld[24] for 3 ½ hides. There is land for three ploughs. In demesne are 2 ploughs; and 12 bordars with 1 plough. There is half a mill[25] rendering 30d and 3 acres of meadow and pasture 10 furlongs long and 1 broad. It was worth 60s; now 100s.

This implies that Aelward, who had held it in the time of King Edward the Confessor, had been dispossessed and Lethelin by then held it of[26] a greater landowner, Ernulf de Hesdin – no doubt a Norman, who was rewarded with land throughout the county including holdings in Keevil, Potterne, Etchilhampton, Cholderton, Deverill and Upton Scudamore[27].

EARLY AGRICULTURE AND LAND TENURE

The first Anglo-Saxon settlers had brought their own farming practices and, before the Normans' arrival in 1066, members of free village communities probably owned the farm land 'in common'.[28] In huge unenclosed fields, each farmer had a number of narrow arable strips, which were not adjacent but scattered and divided from one another by open drains made by the plough.[29]

This 'strip system', which continued under the Normans and lasted to some extent until the inclosures between the sixteenth and the eighteenth centuries, had the advantage of giving each farmer a fair share in

24 Geld was in the nature of a tax or fee.
25 Perhaps the other half was attributed to Great Cheverell.
26 'Of' is a technical usage applying to the Norman instituted land law and means in this context 'from'.
27 *The Wiltshire Domesday*, Editions Alecto (Domesday) Limited, 1989.
28 Cheshire's *Real Property*, 5th edition, p. 23.
29 Known as 'the open field system'. The 'open field' itself might or might not have been surrounded by hurdles, according to need.

the better and worse land – in Little Cheverell of clay, sand and chalk. This helped to bring the villagers together as a community and even the humblest had a voice in agricultural policy. On the other hand, devised for a subsistence economy, the arrangement was only viable as long as the farmer merely produced food for his family and local need and not for the market. A reminder of this system still remains in the 'ridge and furrow',[30] still visible in some of the fields on the east and north of the village.

As late as 1722, the majority of the land in Little Cheverell was still held in strips within larger fields or enclosures called 'furlongs', such as Fursacre, Uptables, and Broadlands furlongs. Furlong was Anglo-Saxon usage for 'a furrow long' and it originally referred to a furrow made by a plough drawn by oxen before turning in a field of ten acres – though it later came to mean the appropriate length in any particular field.

THE MANORIAL SYSTEM

On to the indigenous Saxon way of life the Normans grafted their own more rigid feudal manorial system. Estates with some aspects of manors had come into being in Saxon times and the parish of Little Cheverell, as we have seen, gained its present shape in that early period. The Norman manor was, however, very different from a Saxon one both in concept and its administration. Already by 1086 it was an estate of varying size organised under the aristocratic control of a 'lord'.

The term 'manor' has virtually no relevance to life today and, although 'lordships of the manor' are sometimes put up for auction and sold as commodities, even to residents of the USA or other countries abroad, the title has become an empty one with no meaningful rights or duties remaining. In the past, however, the 'lord of the manor' – whose office had nothing to do with the peerage – was a powerful local figure.

The whole Norman feudal system was built on the concept of service given in return for a corresponding benefit. The major 'tenants' who had been granted large tracts of land by the king were bound, by

30 'Ridge and furrow' refers to an old method of managing arable land in a field, which was ploughed in a special manner to leave a raised rounded strip of land with intermediate open furrows.

‘knight service’, to supply him with arms and men or to perform some other major service for him. Intermediate, or ‘mesne’, tenants were similarly bound to give service to a greater landowner while the rural cultivator’s obligation – called a ‘farm’, the word’s original Anglo-Saxon meaning[31] – was initially simply to sustain the lord of his manor for a given period. Every part of the country came under this regime at different levels and the manorial system governed many aspects of rural life for nine centuries up until 1925.

Poor as well as rich were affected by the Norman innovation and the practical effect on those who farmed the land in Little Cheverell, as everywhere else, was that after 1066 they became ‘villeins’ or ‘bordars’, bound to work on the ‘demesne’ of the lord of the manor for a given period in a form of serfdom. In return they had some degree of protection and the use of land, held as ‘tenants at will’ of the lord, to grow their own crops. It was therefore not surprising that before long the ‘lord of the manor’ came, universally, to be regarded as owner of the soil as well as ‘a man in authority over the district connected with his estate’.

The 1086 Domesday assessment of Little Cheverell at ‘3½ hides’ shows that the arable area was then some 300 acres, the area which could be ploughed by three and a half oxen. Of this the lord retained roughly two thirds – ‘two ploughs’ – as his own ‘demesne’ while one third – ‘one plough’ – was shared between twelve ‘bordars’. The demesne land came later to be known as Manor Farm.

These developments under the Normans have been described as ‘disastrous’ for the villeins[32] as the land they cultivated for themselves was held merely ‘at will’ and they had no legal security of tenure. It is true, however, that arbitrary action by the lord of the manor was limited by mutual interest and custom. The lord needed his land to be worked while the villein had to provide for his family on his own holdings and the custom of the manor could not too lightly be set aside. Nonetheless the lot of even the humblest freeholder was much better than that of the villein because, even as early as Henry II’s time (1154–89), he was protected by the King’s Court. In Little Cheverell, however, there was little or no freehold other than the lord of the manor’s until the nineteenth and twentieth centuries.

31 P. Vinogradoff, *Villainage in England*, pp. 301–2.
32 W. S. Holdsworth, *A History of English Law*.

The lord of the manor of Little Cheverell was a very significant figure to the inhabitants, even though he was rather remote from them, except when he lived in the village himself. During the long years that there was no resident lord, the Lord's steward, the rector and the tenant of the 'demesne farm' would have been far better known among the people. There were only three periods when there was a resident lord of the manor – from the twelfth to the fourteenth centuries, a short period in late Victorian times and another short period in the twentieth century. The longest spell was between 1166 and 1350 when successive members of the Cheverell family lived in a manor house to the south of the church, not far from Hawkswell House. Remaining signs of walls and foundations suggest a large manorial complex and the identification of the site is further confirmed by two fields, formerly called Court Close and Lower Court Close, as well as the discovery there of fourteenth century coins in 2005.

The lord of a small rural manor would not have been able to maintain the style and state of the great lords, but a Mr Albery in an unpublished history of the county quoted in *Cox's Wilts*[33] of 1731 described how a lord might have lived in medieval times in a reference to Great Cheverell:

> The Lords of the Manor were Lords indeed, and lived in their Countries like Petty Kings. They had their Royal Rights belonging to their Seignories, as castles, Boroughs, sent Burgesses to Parliament, and Gallows in the Liberties,[34] on which they could hang malefactors. They kept good Houses, eating at an high Table at the end of their Gothick Halls, where they had an Oriele or little Room on the Side of it, or with a square table. It was perhaps an Oratory in old Time. Jacks are a new invention, poor Boys turned the Spits, licked the dripping-pans, and became but Knaves. The Hearth for their winter Fires was in the Midst of the Halls, whence came the phrase 'round about our coal fires', which might be one of the Christmas Games played in this Hall.

33 Part of his great work 'Magna Britannia et Hibernia, Antiqua et Nova'.

34 Liberties were either ' an authority to do something which would otherwise be illegal or equivalent of "franchise", both as denoting a right and as denoting the place where the right is exercisable.' Earl Jowitt, *The Dictionary of English Law*.

The Halls were hung about with Armour. Destroying of Manors[35] was contemporary with the Dissolution of the Monasteries, which together made the people lawless. There were no inns or ale-houses in those Days; if Travellers had occasion to eat or drink, they went to the Abbies and Priories, where they were allowed Entertainment for three days, if necessity required etc.

However the Cheverell lords of the manor lived, the manorial lands are described on the death of Alexander Cheverell in 1310 at an

Inquisition taken before the King's escheator on 8th November, 4 Edward II[36] by the oath of Peter Clerk, John Foghelere, Geoffrey Moryn, Ralph ate Berne, William Gule, William de Aula, Henry de Woluemere, John Heruy, John de Bacham, Alexander Giffard, Peter Robyn and Richard le Eyr, who say that:

Cheuerel

Alexander Cheuerel was seised in his demesne as of fee on the day he died of the manor of Little Cheuerel, which manor is held in chief of H. de Lacy, Earl of Lincoln, by the service of one knight's fee.

There is one capital messuage, the easements whereof, with the profit of the garden, are worth 20s. per annum; there are on the hill there 414 acres of arable land, worth 103s.5d (3d per acre); and in the marsh and sand 134 acres of arable land, worth 44s.8d (4d per acre); meadow worth 24s; pasture for 40 oxen, worth 26s. 8d (8d per head); pasture for 400 sheep, worth 33s 4d (1d per head). There is one free tenant, who holds one messuage and half a virgate of land, and pays 17s. yearly in equal portions of the 4 principal terms. There are 6 customary tenants, each of who hold one virgate of land and pays 5s yearly. And each of them will work from the feast of the Nativity of St John the Baptist to the feast of St Michael, and the work of each is worth 5s. There are 7 customary tenants there, each of whom holds a quarter of a virgate, paying 40d. Item, the rents of the cottars at the said 20s. in equal portions. The pleas and perquisites are worth one mark per annum. Total £19.5s.0d.

35 He evidently meant the old-fashioned way of running a manor, for manors and the manorial system continued for nearly a further 400 years.
36 The fourth year of the reign of Edward II.

After the middle of the fourteenth century no lord of the manor lived in the village itself until another 600 years had passed. Then in 1889 Walter Pleydell-Bouverie, a son of the Earl of Radnor, came to live at Manor Farm House and, farming 800 acres from there, also held the manor until his death in 1893. After that there was another gap until between 1918 and 1934 Robert Awdry, the last lord of the manor, owned Hawkswell House and lived there.

THE LORDS OF THE MANOR

The tortuous history of the lordship shows how, even if remotely, the village was connected to events and personages of national importance. The manor seems to have passed, first through Maud, the daughter of the Tenant-in-Chief in 1086 Ernulf de Hesdin, and then his granddaughter, Sibyl, to the Earl of Salisbury, who also owned considerable other land in Wiltshire. By 1166 the manor was acquired and held – at least initially of the Earl of Salisbury – by the Cheverell family, who held it for some 200 years over several generations. Whether this family took their name from the parish or not is not known, but by the latter half of the twelfth century Alexander Cheverell held eleven hides of the Earl of Salisbury and by 1237 Sir Alexander Cheverell, who was possibly his son though more likely grandson, held the manor and also became Escheator[37] of Wiltshire in 1246. In about 1260 he was succeeded by his son, Sir John, and then his grandson, another Sir Alexander, who was High Sheriff in 1308–9. Members of the Cheverell family probably lived in the manor house until about 1350 at the time of the Black Death, but after that no one appears to have occupied it and no part of its structure remains standing and visible above ground.

On Sir Alexander's death in 1310, his daughter Joan became his heir, presumably as he had no son, and the manor passed into the hands of the St Lo family. The succession of the lordship after the generations of

37 An office which was abolished in 1660 on the abolition of the Court of Wards and Liveries. The Escheator's duty was to look to escheats, wardships and other casualties involving reversion of an estate to the Crown. Escheats occurred when property was due to revert to the Crown for the lack of an heir to the property or because the person holding the tenancy was convicted of a felony. Jowitt, *The Dictionary of English Law*.

Cheverells was complicated. In the later fifteenth century and throughout the sixteenth and much of the seventeenth centuries the manor was held by the Hungerford family, one of whose members, Sir Thomas Hungerford, was the first recorded Speaker of the House of Commons – sitting as such at the last Parliament of King Edward III in 1377. Both he and his son, Sir Walter Hungerford, were Knights of the Shire for Wiltshire and Sir Walter, who became the first Baron in the time of King Henry V, also became Speaker in 1414.[38]

Sir Walter (1378–1449) was MP for Somerset as well as Wiltshire. Eccentric but, like his father, distinguished, he fought at Agincourt in 1415, was appointed Knight of the Garter, and was later executor of King Henry V's will. When he himself died, he was buried in Salisbury Cathedral – bizarrely in an iron cage which he had himself erected.

A connection between the village and the Hungerford family was briefly re-established on 16 December 1998 when Lady (Ruth) Hawley, High Sheriff of Wiltshire 1998–9, accompanied by the author, attended the commemoration service at St Leonard's Chapel, Farleigh Hungerford, of the 600th anniversary of the death in 1398 of Sir Thomas, the first Speaker. It was an intensely cold evening with a hard frost and conditions were spartan, as heating was proscribed through fear of damage to the medieval frescoes. Nevertheless the Bishop of Bath and Wells, Bishop Jim Thompson, preached undaunted whilst the congregation, however warmly clad, shivered. Fortunately the welcome dinner, which followed, was in a well-heated marquee. Lord (Bernard) Weatherill, who was Speaker of the House of Commons from 1983 to1992, made the principal speech.

The Hungerford family continued to hold the manor of Little Cheverell until 1718 when it was sold by Lord Lexington to Sir Edward des Bouverie, whose descendant was created Earl of Radnor in 1765. Thereafter it was held by the Bouverie family until 1902. In the middle of the nineteenth century the manor was conveyed by the third Earl to his second son Edward Pleydell-Bouverie, who died in 1889 but not before he had left some mark on the village by erecting boundary stones with his initials 'EPB'[39] on them. The manor then passed to Edward's

38 A third Knight of the Shire for Wiltshire, Sir Walter Beauchamp, was Speaker in 1416. J. L. Roskell, 'Three Wiltshire Speakers', *The Wiltshire Archaeological and Natural History Magazine*, CCIV, June 1956, vol. LVI.
39 One was found near East Sands.

elder son Walter (1848–93), who also made his different but benevolent mark on the village economically and socially, when he lived at Manor Farm House.

Edward Pleydell-Bouverie had not lived in the village but it was he who commissioned the architect Ewan Christian in 1865 to design a new Manor House – now part of Dauntsey's School – on the western borders of the Lavington parish and for a time he lived there himself. In 1902 the manor of Lavington together with that of Little Cheverell was sold to Charles Awdry. He could not immediately occupy the Lavington Manor House as it was let to the Marquise de la Valette, whose husband was a descendant of the famous Grand Master of the Knights of Malta who gave his name to Valetta – Jean de la Valette. Nonetheless, from 1909 until 1912 Charles Awdry was able to live in it himself and, being a keen cricketer, laid out a cricket ground – now in the grounds of Lavington School – on which first class cricket matches were played in the early years of the twentieth century.[40] In July 1914 Charles Awdry sold much of the total estate, including Little Cheverell, having already lost all the hill farms by compulsory purchase by the War Office in 1910.

The lordship of the manor of Little Cheverell was offered for sale at the same time as the rest of the Lavington estate, a considerable part of which, including the village, was bought by John Nosworthy. The lordship, however, did not sell for some reason and the manor therefore passed successively to Charles Awdry's two sons, first Major Selwyn Awdry, who was killed in the First World War, and then Colonel Robert William Awdry. Hawkswell House, a substantial neo-Georgian house, was begun in 1914 by Mrs Awdry, the widow of Charles Awdry, and completed by Robert Awdry after the war in 1920. The architect Arthur Campbell Martin, whose work also included the extension to the chapel at the Royal Military Academy, Sandhurst, was a cousin of Mrs Charles Awdry and the builders were Sainsburys of Littleton Panell. No less than thirty-four men were employed to ply their various trades. All the bricks were local and it was a matter of great pride to Charles Turner, then owner of the brickworks in the north of the village, that his yard had supplied them. Hawkswell House was the last house in the village occupied by a lord of the manor. This ended, however, in 1934 when the War Department acquired a considerable

40 Information given to the author by Dick Hurn – aged ninety-two in 2003 – who used to play cricket with Robert Awdry, son of Charles Awdry.

amount of Robert Awdry's land together with the house and the lordship, even though the Awdrys continued to live at Hawkswell for some years as tenants.

In 1941, in the middle of the Second World War, Hawkswell House, which had been taken over by the War Department, was divided into flats for officers' accommodation and so it remained until 1982 when it was sold by the Ministry of Defence for £174,000 to Gaiger Bros. who, having turned it into four civilian flats and two houses, sold them on. As for Robert Awdry and his wife Olive, they lived briefly at Little Cheverell House after leaving Hawkswell in 1940[41] and then at East Croft in Long Street, Devizes, although Olive Awdry later returned to the village and lived at East Sands.

Robert Awdry played a prominent part in Wiltshire affairs and was inter alia Chairman of the County Council and first Chairman of the Wiltshire Victoria County History Committee. When he died in 1949 a very large number of people, including many county and national figures, attended his memorial service at West Lavington church, taken by the Bishop of Bristol, Dr F. A. Cockin, assisted by the Bishop of Sherborne, Dr J. M. Key. In his address on 'the life of Bob Awdry' Dr Cockin conceded that anything he said would pale beside the vivid personal memories of those who had 'shared his many-sided interests, played cricket and shot with him, worked with him on committee and council and come to rely almost daily on his friendship, judgement and leadership'. He also referred to Robert Awdry's ability, kindness and wisdom.

Robert Awdry's sister Helen, who had spent part of her earlier life at Hawkswell, still came to Little Cheverell Church until her death in 1982. Another sister of Robert Awdry, Alethea, married the Revd G. E. Newsom, Master of Selwyn College, Cambridge, and their son, George, became an eminent QC and Bencher of Lincoln's Inn, who lived at Bishop's Cannings. His sister, Margaret Newsom, taught in North Borneo and after her return became headmistress of Holy Trinity School in Great Cheverell. Later marrying Colonel Rupert Wheatley, she was, until her death in 1997, the last member of the Awdry family to retain close connections with the village and, as Treasurer of the PCC, the church. Earlier, the Revd Wilbert Awdry, who was curate of both Little and Great Cheverell, lived on the edge of the parish at Beech

41 From 30 March to 6 September 1940. Information from Greta Taylor from records kept by her father-in-law Clem Taylor.

End House, where he wrote *Thomas the Tank Engine*[42] and thus achieved international fame.

THE TWO CHEVERELLS

Some local people talk of 'Cheverell', which can be confusing – the more so because the villages of Great Cheverell and Little Cheverell have always been distinct and separate entities. Curious as it may appear, by the time of the Domesday Book, when Ernulf de Hesdin held the manor of Little Cheverell, Great Cheverell[43] was connected with the royal manor of Amesbury which was in the hands of the Abbess of the Abbey there. Earlier, however, Amesbury had been granted by William the Conqueror to Earl William fitzOsbern, his Seneschal[44] – a High Steward of the Royal Household with judicial powers – who exchanged farm land at Bowcombe in the Isle of Wight for land in Wiltshire, including Swindon[45] and Great Cheverell. Earl William's land, however, had reverted to the Crown in 1075.

The manor of Great Cheverell continued to be held from that time onwards entirely independently of Little Cheverell, though the Hungerford family held both manors among their lands, and this old dispensation may perhaps help to explain why the strong sense of distinct identity has continued until recent times. Bishop Victor Pike, former Bishop of Sherborne, even felt that he had 'got into hot water' in the Cheverells because he had preached at Little Cheverell before Great Cheverell![46] Nevertheless, despite original different allegiances, other factors – proximity, circumstance, intermarriage and common names – have always bound the two villages together in a special intimacy.

CHANGING NATURE OF LAND TENURE

The era of early villeinage under the Normans was of limited duration and rural people gradually gained new freedoms over the years, helped

42 A series of books for children, starting their popularity in the 1960s.
43 *An Introduction to the Wiltshire Domesday*, Alecto Historical Editions, 1989, pp. 12 and 39.
44 This office was developed particularly in the time of the Norman and the Angevin (Plantagenet) – as well as the French – kings.
45 Then appearing as 'Quintone'.
46 Told to the author by Bishop Pike in about 1984.

by greater independence of mind resulting from individuals' long absences from home in lengthy wars in France and periodic shortage of labour. As early as the late thirteenth century, therefore, lords of some manors began to commute the obligation to give service on the demesne fields into the receipt of monetary rents. Erlestoke, very close to Little Cheverell, was one such. This trend, however, was slowed down in the late thirteenth and early fourteenth centuries when villeins' families multiplied. The resulting competition for available strips of land to cultivate in a manor grew more intense. Lords' bailiffs were able to drive harder bargains to enforce compliance with the villein's obligation to work on the demesne farm.

Then, in 1348 and 1349, the whole country was suddenly devastated by the horror of the Black Death, which killed between a third and a half of the population in rural as well as urban areas. This naturally resulted in an unprecedently severe shortage of manpower on the land with the consequent effects of higher wages and men leaving the villages where they lived.

To combat this, Parliament introduced – more at the instance of smaller landowners and tenant farmers than of the feudal magnates – the Statute of Labourers in 1351, which was re-enacted from time to time. It was designed to keep wages down and to prevent villeins from leaving their own villages. The law was enforced with great harshness, such as branding fugitive villeins on the forehead, and at the same time attempts were made to restore the earlier strict forms of villeinage by reversing the trend towards commuting personal service for rent.

Although these measures were only partially successful, they gave rise to increasing grievances about social ills and disparity between men of different classes. The majority of the rural population were still able to eat and drink comparatively well, but their sense of injustice turned them to local riots, strikes and the revolt led by John Ball in 1360. Discontent continued and culminated in the turbulent and terrible period of the Peasants' Revolt in the east of England in 1381.

The shortage of labour caused by the Black Death had other consequences however. The advantage in negotiation over commutation of labour to payment of rent was, by force of circumstances, returned to individual surviving villeins, who were also often able to incorporate strip holdings left derelict by the death of neighbours into their own. Those who profited in this way were thus transformed into middle class yeomen employing their own labour, while other villeins became landless labourers. Thus new divisions opened up in the countryside between those whose fathers and grandfathers had worked side by side on adjacent strips in the open fields and on the lord's demesne.

INTRODUCTION OF MONETARY RENTS

Nonetheless the fourteenth and fifteenth centuries saw an increasing number of villeins able to save or borrow enough shillings to buy their freedom from serfdom and pay rent for their land holdings. At the same time money came to be used more generally as a result of increasing commercial transactions in wool, woollen cloth and other goods with Flanders, as well as with Aquitaine and Normandy, then held by the English.[47] At a time when the wool trade was growing in importance, those who owned sheep – as some probably did in Little Cheverell – were in an especially strong position to buy their way out of villeinage. About the same time lords of the manor started to hire labour for their own demesne land in place of feudal service, but, when the cost of this grew too high, they began to let even the demesne farm to one of the new emerging yeomen.

COPYHOLD

A rent-paying yeoman farmer remained legally a 'tenant at will' at the 'pleasure' of the lord. In practice, however, his security of tenure was greater than a villein's, because the grant of his lease was recorded in the 'rolls'[48] of the manorial court and he also received a copy of the entry. This procedure gave rise to a new form of tenure termed 'copyhold' which, gradually replacing villeinage, lasted in most rural areas until abolished by the Law of Property Act 1925.

Copyhold leases were often granted for life, or for the lives of two or more members of the same family, and, having no fixed term, gave the tenant the benefit of paying a constant rent over long periods despite

47 P. Vinogradoff, *Villainage in England*.

48 These 'rolls', which recorded land transactions of various kinds such as mortgages, were often very comprehensive and included surveys, maps, notes and 'terriers', detailing boundaries, franchises, wastes, and customs. A terrier was a register or survey of lands setting out the tenures and boundaries. Jowitt, *The Dictionary of English Law*. The term 'Master of the Rolls' derives from the manner in which the court records were originally kept on rolls of parchment.

inflation. He also acquired the further advantage of a new right – not previously enjoyed by villeins – of resort to the king's courts. The changed situation was summed up by the famous jurist and judge Sir Edward Coke:[49]

> Now copyholders stand on sure ground, now they weigh not the lord's displeasure, they shake not at every blast of wind, they eat, drink and sleep securely... For if the lord's anger grow to expulsion, the law hath provided several weapons of remedy: for it is at his election either to sue a sub-poena or an action of trespass... Time hath dealt very favourably with copyholders.[50]

CHANGING NATURE OF LAND TENURE IN LITTLE CHEVERELL

All these developments were reflected even in as small a village as Little Cheverell and villeinage was replaced by varying categories of tenants. These included 'virgaters' who held a 'virgate' or 'verge', an area of from fifteen to thirty acres, and 'customers' whose terms were prescribed by the custom of the manor, which, though not defined in writing, was 'a right established by long use and consent of the ancestors and daily practised'. By 1310, as revealed at the inquisition on the death of Alexander Cheverell mentioned above, there were one 'free tenant' – presumably free of the obligation to work on the lord's demesne – and six 'customers' each holding half of a 'virgate' and seven holding a quarter of a 'virgate' – all very small areas.

In 1341 the demesne land was still far greater than all the other land holdings put together. In 1529 there were fifteen customary tenants and in 1546 five 'customers' and ten tenants with small holdings of land. As late as 1609 'customers' in Little Cheverell were still under obligation to mow and make hay on the demesne farm even though by then most other incidents of feudal obligation had disappeared. In 1682 there were seventeen tenants whose rents totalled £12 per annum and in 1722, of the twenty tenants, seven were cottagers and only five held farms of over 20 acres.

The land in Little Cheverell came to fall into four main categories: first, the common land, in which lord, rector and tenants all had rights 'in common' though this diminished continually from the sixteenth

49 1552–1634
50 *Compleat Copyholder.*

century onwards; secondly, land held under various types of tenancies 'at will', though mainly copyhold; thirdly, the rector's glebe holdings for the maintenance of the church and himself and his family; and fourthly the lord's 'demesne', always the largest area and usually let out on lease for life or a series of lives but without fixed term of years.

The names of particular features of the land which the people cultivated in the parish give some impression of its nature and the exact way in which it was used. Many of these old names – which appear on a fine, detailed map of 1722 – go back to early feudal times when land was held in common and strip cultivation prevailed and they described the nature of the soils – sand, clay and chalk – the whereabouts and usage of land and the occupations of inhabitants. The words 'leaze' and 'mead' meant a lea, field or meadow and in Little Cheverell there were, amongst others: Great Leaze, Long Leaze, Oxen Leaze, Sheephouse (or Shepherd's) Leaze, Lord's Mead.

The Great Leaze, which comprised some sixty acres towards the north of the village, was divided in the sixteenth century into Long Leaze on the west and Oxen Leaze and Sheep Leaze on the east. The Lord's Mead, part of the lord of the manor's own 'demesne' land, was in the Greenlands Farm area a little further north and Shubwell – a term which has survived until now – was formerly a common field in the north west of the parish. North, East and West fields also date from this early era.

Although no marshland remains in the parish, mentions of common rights of pasture in the 'Marsh'– and perhaps reed gathering – occur in documents as late as the eighteenth century. Marsh hedge was presumably a dividing boundary between the marsh and other land. It seems that in earlier days this marsh was created by the permanent or periodical flooding by the Hawkswell stream of the area lying to the west and north of the last of the old cottages on Low Road and straddling the road to Great Cheverell.

The chalk of the uplands is commemorated in names such as White Field and White Road and the clay by the Great Clay, a huge arable field between the escarpment of Cheverell Cliff and Hawkswell. Some land too was particularly associated with the church and glebe, and arable fields lying on either side of Low Road by Shovel Wood were known as 'Upper and Lower Deacons'. A tradition, also about a small pasture field called 'Deacons', is that 'the rent was originally given in bread and cheese for the poor'. There was also a piece of arable land in the open field above the parish called Church Acre, where human bones have been found though no explanation for this has yet been found.[51] Perhaps they were remains from an earlier settlement or even possibly a burial ground during a period of plague such as the Black Death.

In the extreme south of the parish a parcel of land was called Downs, with the Piece, to the north of it, and then various holdings going northwards towards Fore Hill and Cheverell Cliff – also known at one time as Tenantry Hill. To the north of the Great Clay but to the south of the Westbury to West Lavington road (B3098) fields were, as noted above, called Court Close, Lower Court Close, Hawkswell and Hawkswell Fur. Amongst terms which dropped out of use are: Hopes Nine Acres; Hitche Cley; Stoakeaway; Crosse furlong; Picked furlong; Somerfield Cley; Wettlands; Uptables furlong; Doales Oak; Broadlands; Slade furlong; Cleve hedge; Marslong Sherde; Churchland; Littletone hedge; Fury Hill (perhaps Furze); Borden Stile; Little Foxeditche; The Craftes.[52]

There were also a number of other names of local features which, in more recent times when people still seldom went far from home, were on everyone's tongue in a way which they no longer are. Some of the older inhabitants of the village still living, for instance, recall the Green, the Dene, the Clay, Bottom Farm and Bolter's Barn but there were many more, commonly used, names (see Appendix B).

MANORIAL COURT PROCEEDINGS

When leases for money were introduced in place of 'villeinage', the recording of transactions in land became the main business of the lord of the manor's court. This was probably convened in Little Cheverell itself until about 1350, but after that would have been held elsewhere, although a 1783 reference to a 'Court house 49 ft. by 11 ft., supported by oak posts and thatched'[53] in the Rectory grounds is puzzling and might suggest that the manorial court was held there by the lord of the manor's steward by some mutual arrangement with the rector.

51 Answers to interrogatories given by the rector in 1863 for the Collections of Parochial Histories of Wilts.

52 *Wiltshire Glebe Terriers 1588–1827*, ed. Steven Hobbs, Wiltshire Record Society, vol. 56, 2003, p. 79 *et seq.*, 149.

53 *Wiltshire Glebe Terriers 1588–1827*, ed. Steven Hobbs, Wiltshire Record Society, vol. 56, 2003, p. 85.

Surviving records of early court proceedings are patchy and few,[54] but proceedings of the Earl of Radnor's manorial court for the years 1756 to 1828, though brief, are written in legible longhand. They well illustrate the procedure which would have been followed through the centuries.

The court, technically known as the 'Court Baron', was held yearly and nearly all the proceedings took place 'before' the lord's deputy, normally his solicitor, and those mentioned in this capacity are William Pinniger, and later Broome Pinniger, and John Heath, 'Gents'. Each was referred to as 'steward by the rod' and – more registrar than judge – his chief function was 'to receive surrenders' and 'grant admittances' to copyhold lands in the manor, although other sorts of case also cropped up.

The proceedings started with the 'homagers', sometimes called the 'homage jury', who were respected men living in the manor and listed at each court session. They made 'presentments of all things done within the manor to the prejudice of the lord or tenants and to recommend whatever might appear to be advantageous to the lord and not injurious to the tenants'.[55] Such presentments, in 1767 for instance, included : 'that the scouring of the water course – the Hawkswell stream – should be done by the proprietors of the lands adjoining by the following Lady Day and that the scouring of the ditches should likewise be done from New Lane to Long Leaze Gate'. The rolls also record warnings and fines for not maintaining leased property and failure to pay rents.

Another type of presentment is typified by a presentation in 1788 that 'James Newman should serve as Hayward for the year'. The hayward was an officer of the manor, sworn in before the court, with the duty of looking after the boundary fences and also to prevent animals from trespassing on meadows etc.[56]

Originally homagers had to be freeholders but later were usually copyholders. Amongst those from Little Cheverell who exercised this function at various times were James Axford and Thomas Axford, who was referred to in 1768 as maltster 'by virtue of copy of court roll', presumably because he was appointed as such when Bridge House was still a malt mill, possessed by the lord of the manor. Other homagers listed, who tended to be yeoman copyholders, were William Butcher,

54 There are sixteenth-century records for Little Cheverell held in County Archives at Trowbridge, but they are not in very good condition and very difficult for the untutored eye to interpret, owing to the nature of the writing.
55 Jowitt, *The Dictionary of English Law.*
56 Jowitt, *The Dictionary of English Law.*

Thomas Hayward, John Newman, Thomas Wilkins and John and William Crouch.

The majority of entries in the court rolls relate to admissions to, and surrenders of, leases, many of which were for life or the lives of two or more members of a family. However, some entries before the 1802 inclosures also relate to common fields and common arable and cattle grazing rights. Land transactions were invariably recorded as 'by Copy of Court Roll' and 'according to the custom of the manor' and one specific example is a grant of a lease in 1767 in the Axford family 'for the lives of Sarah Axford, John Cumbling Axford and the life of the longest liver of them successively at the will of the lord according to the Custom of the Manor'. Another example was the admission of Jane Marks as tenant of a cottage and orchard 'for the term of her widowhood'. In some cases a 'fine' was payable when a change in tenure was made and the homagers' presentment in 1782 gave notice that a heriot – 'the right to some chattel of a deceased tenant, reserved on a grant or lease of a freehold property'[57] – was due to the lord of the manor on the death of Thomas Axford when John Cumbling Axford succeeded him as copyholder. This was, however, only one example of a number of heriots mentioned in the court rolls.

The particulars of sale of the 2,500-acre Lavington estate in 1914, which included 'practically the entire village' of Little Cheverell, Manor Farm, Greenlands and Cheverell Mill, are revealing on the terms of local leases. Some cottages and land were let on yearly Michaelmas tenancies and others for life or lives and lot 130, for instance, was 'a pair of excellent semi-detached cottages brick built and tiled held by Mrs Abraham Bolter upon lease (not renewable) on her own life, born in 1838, and the life of her son, Abraham Holmes Bolter, born about 1867'.

FREEHOLDERS

Despite the predominance of copyholders, it appears, from the 'Poll Book for Election of Two Knights for the County of Wilts in 1818', that there were already some very small freehold properties in the village. The following are listed as 'Freeholders':

57 *Ibid*. Originally the term meant 'a tribute to the lord of the manor of the horse or habiliments of the deceased tenant in order that they could continue to be used for national defence by each succeeding tenant'. Later it was the right of the lord of the manor to the best beast of a tenant, who died owning an estate of inheritance.

William Richards, the rector
Samuel Munday
John Hatter
John Bolter – listed as a labourer, his property being a house
James Bolter – listed as a brickmaker with a house
James Bolter jun. – listed as a gardener with a house
George Phillips – listed as a labourer with house
George Rideout
James Newman – listed as a labourer with a house
Thomas Chapman – listed as a gardener with a house and land
James Heath – listed as a farmer with a house and land

Thomas Comlyn Axford was also listed as a freeholder with land in Marston though no freehold in Little Cheverell. It was not until 1832 – by virtue of the Reform Act – that copyholders had the right to vote in elections.

By 1873 two members of the Bolter family were listed as freeholders in the Register of Landowners – Abraham Bolter with 11 acres, 1 rood and 34 perches with an assessed rental of £80.14.0 and Samuel Bolter with 2 acres, 2 roods and 31 perches.

COMMON LAND AND INCLOSURES

Until the end of the eighteenth century a considerable amount of village land had, from pre-Norman times, been held in common for pasturing animals. Such areas included the meadow known as Shubwell – sometimes latterly called Shrubwell – in the north west of the parish; the Great Leaze of over 60 acres; Long Leaze of 22 acres; and the marsh of some 60 acres 'straddling the road across the parish from Great Cheverell', where there may also have been common rights of gathering reeds. However, the process of inclosing common land began in 1526, when the farmer of the demesne farm, evidently one of the Warde family as tenant of the lord of the manor, inclosed Great Leaze, extinguishing the rights of pasture previously enjoyed there by the rector and other tenants. This was naturally disputed but, although some of those dispossessed regained entrance to the former common by force, the validity of the inclosure was upheld[58] and the Great Leaze was divided into Sheephouse and Oxen Leaze. The object of the inclosures was to

58 *Victoria County History*, vol. X, p. 56.

create more efficient agricultural units and this process continued to gain momentum.

Thus part of the common land in the marsh may also have been inclosed in the sixteenth century and then, between 1671 and 1704, the remaining common rights of the rector and tenants in the rest of the marsh were extinguished with the land inclosed being divided out. The common pastoral rights of tenants on Long Leaze, the downland and common fields were also slowly extinguished as individual tenancies, which had previously carried common privileges with them, fell in.

The final phase of inclosures of common land, and the concomitant final extinction of nearly all common rights, in Great as well as Little Cheverell came at the turn of the eighteenth and nineteenth centuries. An Act of Parliament was required to achieve this and the preamble to the Inclosure Act of 1797 set out the rationale: 'Whereas the several parishes of Great and Little Cheverell in the County of Wiltshire adjoin and within the said parishes are several Open and Common Fields and Downs, Common Meadows, Common Pastures and other Open and Common Lands and Grounds which lie intermixed and dispersed and in their present situation cannot be cultivated and improved to the best advantage. ...'

Apart from the object of making agriculture more productive, the intention was to rationalise and consolidate the glebe lands of the rector of Little Cheverell.

Three commissioners were therefore appointed to carry out the necessary further division and allocation of the common land in both Cheverells. They were Richard Richardson, Francis Webb and Richard Davis, justices of the peace, with William Tubb as surveyor. After their inquiry they certified that in their judgement 'a full equivalent and compensation (Quantity, Quality, Situation and Convenience)' was achieved 'to one full 5th part of all and singular the Arable lands by the said Act intended to be divided and allotted and of the old Inclosures being Arable lying in the said parish of Little Cheverell'.

In contrast with sixteenth-century inclosures, the consent of all interested parties was obtained and the award document,[59] together with the accompanying maps, reveal the meticulous care with which the commissioners discharged their duty. The award also dealt with roads,

59 Now held in the County Records Office for the County of Wiltshire (EA63).

both public and private, and some definitions of parcels of land related to the road now designated as B3098, known then as the 'Turnpike Road' (showing that it was then a toll road). The final document – deposited in the office of the clerk of the peace on 15 May 1803 – was signed not only by the commissioners but by the Earl of Radnor, as lord of the manor of Little Cheverell, the Bishop of Salisbury, the rectors of Little and Great Cheverell (respectively the Revds William Richards and Richard Laurence), Thomas Burnell, James Walker, Abraham Newman, H. P. Wyndham, Joshua Smith and Job Gibbs.

THE SMALLER TENANCIES

Reverting to events before this, 141 acres of the land – still held in 1767 by some tenants in traditional arable strips – were incorporated into Axford's Farm by virtue of a rearrangement and inclosure of lands agreed upon with the Earl of Radnor as lord of the manor. The basis of this incorporation is not entirely clear but it presumably came about as a result of some leases being surrendered on the death of a tenant or by agreement with compensation of some sort. Although customary copyhold tenancies of smaller areas also continued, the new arrangement illustrated the general trend towards larger holdings and Thomas Axford became the copyhold leaseholder of a large area of land, which came to be known as Axford's Farm, in the Greenlands Farm area. As such he became the tenant of one of the only three large farms in the village, the other two being the demesne farm and the Parsonage Farm.

Following the 1802 award and through much of the nineteenth century and the first years of the twentieth, the lord of the manor continued to own most of the overall freehold of the land.

THE PARSON'S GLEBE

The earliest record of a small area of glebe land and of tithes – 'payments due by the inhabitants of a parish for the support of the parish church and generally payable to the parson of the parish'[60] – was in 1341. By 1582 some of the rector's glebe had been consolidated into larger holdings than he had previously held in his separated strips. At that time his house stood on or near the site of Little Cheverell House

60 Jowitt, *The Dictionary of English Law*, p. 918.

(the former Rectory) and his holding included farm buildings including a glebe barn,[61] 80 acres of arable land, 4½ of meadow and pasture and feeding rights on the common land for 130 sheep, 19 'beasts' and a bull. If all his separated holdings had then been worked as a single farm – which was probably not the case – it would have been the next largest after the demesne farm and figures for 1609 show that the glebe was valued at £40 compared with £150 for the demesne farm and £128 for the combined holdings of the other tenants.

Considerable light is thrown on the nature of glebe holdings, particularly before the inclosures, by 'terriers' produced by the incumbents at various times – one of considerable length and detail, undated but definitely late sixteenth or early seventeenth century. Other such 'terriers' followed in 1671, 1705, 1780 and 1783.

The earliest 'terrier' demonstrates how closely the rector's small parcels all over the parish brought him into contact with his parishioners:

> Arable land in the North field: 2 acres together shooting [running] towards Littleton hedge, bounded with ½ acre of John Stille, and 1 acre of John Hollowaye; ½ acre in the same furlong bounded with ½ acre of William Cumlyn and 1 acre of Nicholas Smithe; in the same furlong 3x½ acres together bounded with 1 acre of William Coaltstone and ½ acre of William Doale; 2 acres more together shooting as the last, bounded on one side with 1 acre of William Coaltstone, and ½ acre of wid. [widow] Warde.

Grazing rights in the common land were strictly defined by numbers of beasts allowed, location and the time of year when it was permissible to graze them in accordance with custom. So, for instance, the rector had: '4 rother[62] beasts or two horses feeding in the common called the Marsh from the Invention of the Cross[63] [3 May] or 10 May until the breach of the barley field, then into the barley, wheat and rye fields as long as they shall hold, then into the Marsh again until St Thomas's day [21 December]. 14 rother beasts feeding in Longleaze from Whitsun Eve, formerly, now 1 June, until the breach of the fields'.

61 Pulled down in 1898.

62 Also called rudder – meaning oxen, cows, steers, heifers and similar horned animals.

63 *Sic.* 3 May was celebrated by the Church in reference of the reputed finding of the true cross by Helena, the mother of the Roman Emperor Constantine in AD 326.

Apart from the grazing, other rights which the rector enjoyed as part of his glebe were: trees and fern with the under frith [common land]; any furzes[64] and fern in the lower Cliffe; a plot of furzes in the Marsh; and linchets next to the arable land.

The 1767 rearrangement of agricultural holdings and practice augmented the rector's glebe by 57 acres lying to the north of the Rectory itself together with a further seven-acre piece of land known as Fuzzy's Hill – or Furze Hill – given in compensation for his previous common feeding right on Long Leaze for 80 sheep.

The aim in the Inclosure Act of 1797 and the award of 1802 of rationalising the rector's lands was mainly achieved by exchanges of land belonging to the Earl of Radnor and the rector in both Cheverells. As a result all the rector's holdings were concentrated in Little Cheverell itself rather than partially scattered outside the parish and he gained more land in compensation for the final abolition of his tithes. Thus Parsonage Farm became a single unit of over 200 acres, all lying in the east of the parish stretching from north of the Great Cheverell to Devizes road to the south of Fore Hill above Cheverell Cliff. The abolition of tithes had a lasting effect on property holding in the village and, when the village houses were sold with the rest of the Lavington estate in 1914, they were advertised in the sale particulars as 'tithe free' in contrast to property offered at the same time in neighbouring places like West Lavington, where tithes were still payable to the parson.

Between 1802 and 1860 the Glebe was divided into two farms each of about 93 acres of principally arable land – one in the north of the village and the other in the south. The southern part was leased out to smallholders while the lease of the northern farm, known as Glebe or Parsonage Farm, was granted to members of the Bolter family. Samuel Bolter, who was described as dairyman and shopkeeper, acquired this lease and from 1860 lived in Glebe Farm House, also farming, according to the census of 1871, 100 acres of glebe as well as some demesne land. At the same time he played his part in church affairs as rector's

64 The usefulness of furze in the home is also illustrated by the old West country song, which shows it had a commercial value:

> 'There was an old man and he lived in the West
> And his trade was a-selling of broom, green broom.
> He had but one son and his name, it was John,
> And he lyed abed till 'twas noon bright noon,
> And he lyed abed till 'twas noon.'

churchwarden for sixteen years from 1862 to 1878. In 1879 Abraham Bolter took over this farm from his cousin and, like him, was also churchwarden between 1880 and 1888. This, however, was not the full extent of his commitment for he also farmed Furze Hill, the lease of which he had inherited from his father Isaac. Although the Bolters' prominence in the village then declined, Abraham's son – another Isaac – continued to farm in Little Cheverell until his death in 1921.

Between 1886 and 1916 the northern glebe farm was broken up and leased out as smaller holdings. Frank Beaven acquired South View Farm as one of them while Furze Hill and Hillside Farms were held by members of the Turner family, who had taken over the brickworks around the turn of the nineteenth century from the Bolters. Glebe Farm house remained the centre of a single farm, of which one of the tenants was Edmund Bazell, whose name at this time was sometimes attached to what was otherwise known as Bolter's Barn.

The glebe land was farmed in this way for the rector's maintenance and upkeep of the church until 1916 when it was all sold on Thursday 24 August at the Bear, Devizes by direction of the rector, the Revd H. P. Margesson. The particulars were advertised as 'very valuable Glebe Lands' consisting of 202 acres in 4 lots.

Lot 1 was the 'valuable freehold and tithe free' farm of 102 acres, 0 roods[65] and 12 perches, to which a curious proviso was attached. The rector as lessor had agreed to provide a pond on the hill as well as fencing material up to the value of £100 and the purchaser of the lot was required to indemnify the vendor in respect of this peculiar obligation. It was the man already in occupation of this lot as lessee, John Nosworthy, who bought it and at the same time he acquired the Glebe Farm House.

Lot 2 was 'A stretch of fertile sand land, reaching from Little Cheverell adjoining the Rectory and Road to Littleton Panell (in a ring fence) to the high ground overlooking the Railway and West Lavington G.W.R. station' consisting of 74 acres 0 roods and 26 perches let in numerous allotments and small holdings – together with the shooting, let for £2.10s.

65 Common usage as a measure of land in the past. It denotes a quarter of an acre and contains forty square perches or 1,200 square yards. Its usage is illustrated by the words of Oliver Goldsmith in his poem 'The Deserted Village':

'There was a time ere England's griefs began
When every rood of ground maintained its man.'

Lot 3 was 'the very valuable Brick Yard and Field adjoining' comprising 8 acres, 3 roods and 25 perches. Lot 4 consisted of 'Very valuable small holdings and 5 rich pasture fields'. The tenants of this were 'Mr J. Turner, the Messrs Turner, Mr Phillips and Mr Beaven'.

John Wilfred Nosworthy inherited his father's title to Glebe Farm, house and the greater part of the land, sixty-five acres of which were compulsorily acquired by the War Department in 1934, and, on the younger Nosworthy's death in 1973, it was acquired by Alan Harley from his executors.

A tenant of the glebe was the central figure in a small nineteenth-century village drama. 'Farmer Lennard', who held a tenancy for his own lifetime and that of his wife with reversion to the rector, had what contemporary villagers called a 'grievous falling-out' with either the Revd John Fishlake or the Revd William Nicholls.[66] At the time he was unmarried but, though he was old, he decided to 'spite' the rector by marrying his serving maid in order to keep him out of his reversion for some years. The farmer was in fact near the end of his days but the rector, in true Christian spirit, conducted the marriage ceremony at his bedside and subsequently made no complaint about the new Mrs Lennard staying on as a widow in the house for many more years.

THE DEMESNE, MANOR FARM, ALSO CALLED LITTLE CHEVERELL FARM

The demesne farm, which in 1086 covered two thirds of the cultivable land, was always by far the most significant in the village. Whether farmed by the lord of the manor directly with a bailiff or let on lease it always provided the main source of employment. Throughout the centuries, therefore, the centre of farming operations in the village lay around where Manor Farm House, which is curiously close to Glebe Farm house, now stands. By 1310 the demesne farm consisted of 414 acres of upland and 134 acres of arable lowland with 12 acres of meadow and pasture for 40 oxen and 400 sheep. This included certain rights in the common land shared with the rector and other tenants. In 1341, when the Cheverell family apparently still held the manor in the

66 'Little Cheverell Village History.' It is possible that the farmer's name was Leonard, but it appears as 'Lennard' in this manuscript, which also does not mention the year.

village itself, the demesne still far exceeded the extent of all the other land holdings put together. It was at that stage probably 'in hand' under the direct control of a bailiff and not leased out.

The practice of granting leases of the demesne land, however, was well established from at least the fifteenth century, and in 1487 John Warde was already the tenant. Three generations of the Warde family in fact held the lease, which would have been copyhold, and when John died he was succeeded by his son William Warde, who in turn was succeeded by his son, another John. The tenure of the Wardes was ended in 1577 on the death of the younger John.

By 1600 the total land farmed in the village had increased and consisted of some 600 acres of arable; 120 acres of meadow and inclosed pasture; 165 acres of upland pasture and 52 acres of commonable lowland pasture. The demesne itself consisted of 260 acres of arable, 18 acres of meadow, and 173½ of pasture (103 upland and 73½ lowland). The demesne's arable land was already by then apparently no longer intermingled with the land of the rector and other tenants. It consisted instead of three parts of roughly equal acreage – the Great Clay lying between the village and Fore Hill; Fore Hill itself; and the land to the south as far as the old Bath to Salisbury road.[67]

From 1606 for over a hundred years Manor Farm, as the demesne land will from now on be termed for convenience, was leased to members of the Long family, who, though prominent as landowners elsewhere in Wiltshire, did not hold the lordship of manor itself which remained in the possession of the Hungerford family. The lease would have been on a copyhold basis and Thomas Long was the first member of the family to hold it. On his death in 1654 it passed to his son John, who himself died in 1676. After John Long's death, his widow Eleanor was able to benefit from the terms of the lease which extended her tenure till the end of her life, although she in fact exchanged her rights for an annuity in 1719. As was usual at the time, the rent remained constant over the whole long period of the family's tenure. Thomas Long and John Long, who were both buried in Little Cheverell churchyard, were men of distinction and both became in their turn High Sheriff of Wiltshire.

The purchase of the manor by Sir Edward des Bouverie in 1718 resulted in considerable changes in the structure of farm holdings in the

67 *Victoria County History*, vol. X, p. 56.

whole village. Manor Farm was taken 'in hand' until 1722 – the year in which John Edgar prepared his map of the village lands for Sir Edward – but after that it was let at a rack rent, a rental more beneficial to the owner and representing the 'full annual benefit of the property'. Similarly copyhold leases of other manorial lands, which were previously let on favourable customary terms, were, as occasion offered, turned into leases at rack rents.

After the award of 1802 and the final ending of strip cultivation, there were three large landholdings in the village. The Manor Farm lands occupied virtually all the land in the west and extreme south while Axford's Farm – held, as we have seen, on copyhold lease by Thomas Axford from the Earl of Radnor – occupied most of the extreme north centred on Greenlands Farm. The rector held nearly all the remaining land, all in the east of the parish.

Little change is recorded in the nineteenth century until 1860, when the Earl of Radnor introduced further changes to the farming pattern. The manor farm lands were then split into three farms: Little Cheverell with a reduced acreage, Mill Farm and Greenlands Farm, although Little Cheverell Farm remained by far the largest with 589 acres of arable, 116 acres of lowland and 50 acres of upland grazing. It embraced all the manor land south of the Westbury–West Lavington road (B3098) including New Zealand farm, the farm house and buildings of which were erected between 1860 and 1886. This strange name came into use at a time when British people were settling in New Zealand itself and was used – fancifully – to describe the farm's remoteness, at the very southern edge of the parish, from the centre of village life. The road to it was also steep and a team of fifteen horses was required to move a threshing machine up to it.[68] Bottom Farm, with its two cottages erected in 1860, was also part of this southern manorial land.

Just as the Axfords became prominent at the end of the eighteenth century, so in the nineteenth members of the Bolter family not only ran the brickworks and held the lease of Glebe Farm as recounted above but acquired the tenancy of Greenlands Farm, which was still part of the manorial lands. Richard William Bolter, the son of Samuel, held the tenancy of this farm between 1875 and 1880 and, like his father, was also churchwarden – though only from 1878 to 1880. He then left the

68 Testimony of old villager taken for the 'History of Little Cheverell'.

village to farm elsewhere and, in 1882, Charles Bolter took over from him as tenant of Greenlands Farm, which came to be known colloquially as Bolters Farm, proving himself a successful dairy farmer with between 67 and 111 acres of land at different times.[69]

Members of the Coleman family succeeded the Bolters as tenants and they continued as such after Henry William Hooper purchased the freehold of Greenlands Farm in 1914, at the time when the whole of the Lavington estate was sold. In addition to the regular work on the farm itself, Greenlands was used to pen sheep from the Downs around Imber before consignment on the railway from the nearby Lavington station or being driven to market in Devizes.[70] This farm was sold in 1965 to David Matthew, solicitor to Lloyds of London, whose wife Jo was active in the village, and subsequent owners have been Mr and Mrs O'Gorman and now in 2007 Judith Bredin.

Manor Farm had thus remained the property of the lord of the manor right up to 1914. When John Nosworthy bought it at that point, the era of more modern farming began but it continued to be, as it had always been – on whatever terms it might have been farmed – a constant and central feature of village life.

FARMING AND LOCAL ECONOMY: DAIRYING

The use of the lower-lying land changed periodically, largely according to economic circumstances, and a striking instance of this was when dairy farming had its vogue in the later nineteenth century. From 1886 onwards a great deal of arable lowland was turned into pasture, initially to provide for the needs of the Little Cheverell Dairy started by Walter Pleydell-Bouverie. As resident lord of the manor, he had Manor Farm 'in hand', living at the farm house from 1889 until his death in 1893, and his dairy business was very successful. It not only gave a boost to local employment but gained a wide reputation as it supplied fine butter and cream to the London market. Four large 'Bs' – standing for 'Bouverie's Best British Butter' – enabled the brand to be easily recognised and consignments, packed in locally made crates, were

69 'Labourers, Brickmakers, Churchwardens and Farmers – The Story of the Bolter family from Little Cheverell in Wiltshire from 1550 to 1962' by Richard Bolter 1998. Typed private manuscript.
70 Information from members of the Hooper family.

dispatched daily by train from Devizes Station.[71] The by-products were turned to local use and whey and skim milk from the dairy were used to feed pigs in the farm's piggery on the west of the parish. It was from this that Piggery Cottages took their name.

The operation was conducted from what is now Pillar Box Cottage and Bridge House[72] but was finally closed down in 1896–7. Little Cheverell Dairy was nevertheless one of the original dairies to form Wilts United Dairies Ltd, which in its turn later formed part of a countrywide business, United Dairies Ltd. The memory of the dairy nonetheless persisted locally as, for a while after the closure, the two premises were known as Dairy Cottages.

SHEEP REARING

For countless generations thousands of sheep grazed on the great open spaces of Salisbury Plain above Little Cheverell and sheep rearing was a very important aspect of local life. Sheep had been kept on the Plain from Roman and even earlier times, and in 'the days of its glory sheep cropped the turf' of the 'rolling acres of rough downland grasses dotted with attractive small flowers of the chalk'. Everything, however, began to change in the first half of the twentieth century and already by the 1920s sheep were fast disappearing from the Plain.

The process of converting the land to arable farming began before the First World War but was accelerated by the increasing availability of chemical fertilisers to make corn growing viable and the necessity for home food production in the Second World War.[73] The breaking up of the ancient sheep-grazed turf was, however, greatly regretted by the naturalist W. H. Hudson who also lamented 'the destruction of the ancient earth-works, especially of the barrows, which is going on all over the downs, most rapidly where the land is broken up by the plough'. He wondered, in 1910, 'what our descendants ... will say of us and our incredible carelessness in the matter' and reflected that 'it would not be pleasant to have our children's and children's children's

71 At that period Devizes was on the main line. The realignment of the line came at the turn of the nineteenth and twentieth centuries.

72 Now belonging to Mrs Helena Warnock and Mr and Mrs J. Weyland respectively.

73 Michael Marsham, *A Wiltshire Landscape*, Countryside Books and the Council for the Protection of Rural England, 1984, p. 14.

contemptuous expressions sounding in our prophetic ears'! Apart from the plough, the acquisition in 1943 of 103 acres of downland in the south of the parish for the Larkhill firing ranges also had its effect on old practices on the Plain.

Although grazing land, therefore, gradually gave place to grain, some sheep still remained to give fertility to the fields and as an integral part of the crop rotation system. John Wilfred Nosworthy followed his father in continuing sheep farming, although economic factors ultimately drove him to give up his two flocks.[74] Similarly in neighbouring Imber, where Henry Hooper of West Lavington kept two flocks of 500, sheep farming continued well into the latter half of the twentieth century. His wife described how things were managed on their farm.[75] The ewes were minded by a shepherd on the downs by day and folded in hurdles on the arable land at night, while the lambs were left in the sheep fold. Crops were rotated on the four arable parts of their farm so that wheat might be grown on the first part; barley or oats on the second; swedes and kale, sown in June, on the third part, known as 'new field'; and rape, turnips and vetches for sheep feed on the fourth part – 'old field'.

BREEDS OF SHEEP

Improved breeding of sheep came about when the Romans ruled Britain and they introduced a superior variety by crossing the indigenous 'Soay', which was small agile and hardy, with southern Italian animals which produced fine white fleeces.[76] Further types were introduced over the years until the old Wiltshire breed came to dominate. Of their demise in their turn in the earlier part of the nineteenth century, W. H. Hudson wrote:[77]

> As a naturalist I must lament the loss of the Old Wiltshire breed of sheep, although so long gone. Once it was the only breed known in Wilts, and extended over the entire county; it was a big

74 Reminiscences of Catherine Nosworthy.

75 Article entitled 'Sheep Farming in the 20th Century', chapter 3 of *Pastoral Pedigree* by G. E. Evans.

76 Edward Rutherford, *Sarum*, Arrow Books, 1988, p. 322.

77 W. H. Hudson, *A Shepherd's Life*, Futura Publications Ltd. First edition 1910.

animal, the largest of fine wooled sheep in England, but for looks it compared badly with modern downland and possessed, it was said, all the points which a breeder, or improver, was against. Thus its head was big and clumsy, with a round nose, its legs were long and thick, its belly without wool, and both sexes were horned. Horns, even in a ram, are an abomination to the modern sheep farmer in Southern England. Finally it was hard to fatten. On the other hand it was a sheep which had been from of old on the bare open downs and was modified to suit the conditions, the scanty feed, the bleak, bare country, and the long distances it had to travel to and from the pasture ground. It was a strong, healthy, intelligent animal but, when the South Downs breed was introduced during the late 18th century, the farmer viewed it with disfavour; they liked their old native animal, and did not want to lose it. But it had to go in time, just as in later times the South Down had to go when the Hampshire Down took its place – the breed which is now universal, in South Wilts at all events.

Though a solitary flock of the pure-bred old Wiltshire sheep existed in the county as late as 1840, the breed disappeared so completely that later shepherds had often not even heard of it. At a later stage the Dorset Down and the Hampshire Down came to predominate.

John Nosworthy, whose success in sheep breeding in the first decades of the twentieth century was considerable, was not one of those who had any inhibitions over the size of his ram's horns and proudly showed photographs of those well-endowed in this respect – probably Hampshire Downs – which he sold at Weyhill sheep fair[78].

SHEEP FOLDS AND LAMBING PENS

Lambing pens for folding sheep had to be sturdy and the Sperrin family were among those in the village with a good reputation for making the necessary hurdles. The materials came from the greenwood workers who did the coppicing.[79] The pens were erected on high ground to avoid the wet – usually on the 'old field', next to the swedes, and close both to the barley straw ricks from the previous year and the hay ricks

78 Reminiscences of Catherine Nosworthy.
79 'Our Changing Countryside' – article by Robert Harvey in *Wiltshire Life*, April 2005.

of the 'new field'. The fold containing the pens was constructed of adjoining hurdles held together by strong posts of ash or hazel called 'vossils', lashed together with loops of tarred twine known as 'raves'. The lines of hurdles formed three sides of a square enclosure, while the fourth side was closed by a double row of hurdles packed with straw. The lambing pens, each holding a ewe and her lamb as soon as born, were built around the inside perimeter of the three sides built of hurdles. A thatched roof, supported by slanting poplar poles reaching beyond the hurdles on the outside to give the structure strength against strong winds, covered the pens and overhung a space beyond. Thus the shepherd was able to walk round under cover and tend his ewes in the dry.

The rest of the fold was divided into two parts by a double row of hurdles, with straw packed between them to give warmth, and one inclosure held the in-lamb ewes and the other the ewes with their lambs after they came out of the individual pens. Each inclosure was furnished with a trough of water filled from a horse-drawn barrel, troughs of linseed and cotton cake – produced from the bye-products of the soap-making industry – and hay in feeding cages. The lambing season lasted about six weeks beginning each January or February with Hampshire Down sheep first as, maturing early, they produced lambs in time for Easter. Once the lambing season was over, the pen was pulled down – as a precaution against disease.[80] The danger of this is witnessed by numerous historical records, of which just two examples may be quoted. In 1389 'scab and sickness [was] very prevalent' among sheep and in 1766 there was 'great rot in sheep'.[81]

SHEPHERDS

The lives of the very long line of shepherds living in Little Cheverell were undoubtedly arduous, exposed as they were to long periods of wet and cold in winter. The lot of their families was also demanding. For instance, even in the earlier years of the twentieth century, one young schoolgirl in the village, who would have been less than fourteen years

80 Description by Mrs Hooper.
81 *Records of the Season, Prices of Agricultural Produce and Phenomena Observed in the British Isles*, collected by T. H. Baker, Fellow of the Meteorological Society, Simpkin, Marshall and Co., Warminster.

of age, not only looked after the younger children, after their mother died young, but also prepared the meals. In addition, she took her father's lunch up to him on the Plain between the end of morning school and the resumption of lessons in the afternoon.[82]

Of the general character of shepherds, A.G. Street[83] cautioned in the 1930s that, though they never tired of studying their sheep, they were 'autocratic' even with their own employers. He therefore summed up his recommendations: 'Shepherding qualifications being almost equal, choose a cheerful shepherd.' Shepherds were renowned for their toughness and resilience and sometimes remained in their jobs for very long periods, even sixty years. One such man was described by W. H. Hudson. Through long exposure in early life, he had developed rheumatic fever and permanent lameness after catching a chill, but nonetheless remained devotedly in his job for another fifty years. A shepherd was marked not only by his character but also by his dress. It was distinctive: typically he carried a crook, wore a smock, often lightly embroidered, and had a broad hat on his head. He was also addicted to song, also using his voice to control his sheep. Some would even command their dogs to chase the sheep from the path of the oncoming Salisbury coach so that it did not have to slow down.

In past hard times shepherds were sometimes tempted, out of desperation to feed their families, to steal a sheep or connive with one farmer to steal from another. It was, however, a very risky business. For, even as late as the first part of the nineteenth century, sheep stealing was a capital offence. The judges themselves tended to regard it as 'of no great moral turpitude', but such was the severity of the law that many poor men were sentenced to death for it at the Assizes in Salisbury. Increasingly, however, the prerogative of mercy came to be exercised by the Crown and the sentences of death were commuted into transportation to Australia or Tasmania. Of those transported by ships from Portsmouth or Plymouth, some were never heard of again, while others no doubt made good in the Antipodes.

Two well-known shepherds who kept John Wilfred Nosworthy's sheep were Percy Baker, who was in charge of the flock at Little Cheverell, and 'Snowy' Chapman, who kept the flock at Tilshead, living alone there in a hut on wheels with his black and white collies.

82 Recounted in the 1950s and brought to the attention of the author.
83 A. G. Street, *Farmer's Glory*, Faber, 1932.

The last shepherd to live in the village was another employee of John Wilfred Nosworthy – George Cox, father of William ('Bill') Cox and father-in-law of Olive Cox, who still lived in Little Cheverell in 2006.

THE GREAT BUSTARD

Until the first part of the nineteenth century, the Great Bustard (*Otis Tarda*) shared the lonely plain above Little Cheverell with the shepherds. This greatest of British land birds was at one time plentiful on Salisbury Plain and Wiltshire was probably its last breeding ground in England. The last sightings, however, were in 1871 and 1872 and after that it definitely became extinct. Nonetheless it did survive in heraldry and the College of Arms in 1937 granted Wiltshire a crest: 'On a wreath of the colours, a Bustard, wings elevated and addorsed, proper'. In 1967 a badge was also granted to the county: 'On a rounded barry of eight argent and vert a Bustard, wings addorsed, proper'.

The real bustard, when it existed, could be four feet in height and weigh forty pounds, with head and neck bluish grey; back and upper breast buff orange; and underparts white. Its olive-coloured eggs were larger than those of a swan. John Aubrey in the latter half of the seventeenth century was enthusiastic about this splendid bird, noting that it was then very numerous, especially in the fields above Lavington. Its meat, however, was much coveted and, for this in particular, it was hunted to eventual extinction. As early as 1801 John Britton in *The Beauties of Wiltshire* noted that 'the murdering tube of the sportsmen and the pilfering hand of the shepherd have nearly exterminated the whole race'.[84]

The bustard was not normally regarded as aggressive but two strange cases of such behaviour were reported – in its declining days – by the schoolmaster at Tilshead in an article in the *Gentleman's Magazine* in 1805. The more dramatic of the two incidents was described in detail:

> A man about 4 o'clock this morning on some day in 1801 was coming from Tinhead to Tilshead when near a place called Askings Penning, one mile from Tilshead, he saw over his head a large

84 James Thomas, 'The Great Bustard in Wiltshire: Flight into Extinction?', in *The Wiltshire Archaeological and Natural History Magazine*, vol. 93, 2000, p. 63.

bird, which afterwards proved to be a bustard. He had not proceeded far before it lighted on the ground immediately before his horse, which it showed an inclination to attack, and in fact very soon began the onset. The man alighted and, getting hold of the bird, endeavoured to secure it and, after struggling with it nearly an hour, succeeded and brought it alive to the house of Mr Bartlett, at Tilshead, where it continued till the month of August, when it was sold to Lord Temple for the sum of thirty one guineas.[85]

It is heartening to note that a scheme to restore the bustard to the Plain was launched in 2004 by David Walters, chairman of the Salisbury-based Great Bustard Group, and Karen Ray. Thirty three-week-old chicks were imported from the Saratov region in Russia, which has the only remaining sustainable population of the bird, and this attempt to reclaim the species for its old habitat in Wiltshire has continued with further imports of chicks.

DEW PONDS

Essential to the rearing of sheep on the downs above Little Cheverell were dew ponds which, though far from rivers, streams and springs, hardly ever failed even in severe drought. They were not chance affairs and the hand of man was required either to dig a complete new one or to improve a natural site and make it watertight.

The nearest dew pond was beside Bolter's (or Bazell's) Barn on Fore Hill and it was used not only for sheep and but also for watering farm horses when working in that area. Children from the village also liked to go there to catch tadpoles and other forms of pond life.[86] A sadder story is associated with it for Joseph Collins, who lived at Yew Tree Cottage,[87] was locally believed to have committed suicide there on 21 June 1927 by drowning himself.[88] His daughter, Eva Collins,

85 Sir Richard Colt Hoare, *The Ancient History of Wiltshire*, vol. I, 1912, p. 95. Republished in 1975 by EP Publishing Ltd., in collaboration with Wiltshire County Library.
86 Recollections of Greta Taylor, recorded by the author on 19 July 2004.
87 Later called Holly Cottage, the home of Mr and Mrs 'Bill' Palmer.
88 His body was carried down from the pond by the path, which, passing the gatehouse of Hawkswell House, was then known as Fitch's Lane. Information given to the author by Ken and Greta Taylor in 2003. It later fell into disuse and, although marked on eighteenth-century maps, was never formally adopted as a footpath.

continued nevertheless to live in the cottage until her death on 22 June 1979.[89]

Despite the name, it was mainly fog or mist, together with rain, which filled the ponds rather than dew. A great deal of water was produced by the condensation, activated by a tree or large bush adjoining the pond, and Edward Martin[90] described the phenomenon: 'Summer fogs are very common at night on the high downs; the people who go to bed and get up at normal hours do not know of them. These fogs are so wet that a man riding up on the hills at 4.0 am may find his clothes wringing wet from the fog and every tree dripping water.' The actual dew on the grass produced a considerable amount of moisture for the sheep, and men who went to work very early in the morning used to wear 'dew-beater boots'.

Shepherds would therefore wait high on the downs, as sunrise broke through the haze, to identify the best place for any new dew pond – often in an existing hollow. Who made the nearest dewpond to the village, and how, is not known but the traditional skills for constructing dew ponds were maintained in a few local families – the Smith family and a Mr Baker of West Lavington and the Cruse family of Imber among them.[91] Baker's method of working has been recorded:[92]

> First a layer of clay is carefully kneaded and beaten down with much force on the bare chalk. Over this is spread and carefully smoothed out a layer of freshly slaked lime three or four inches thick (to keep out the worms); on this is laid a layer of straw to protect the lime, and over all, six inches of chalk rubble to keep cattle from treading and breaking the clay pudding.

Cattle and sheep, however, were apparently sometimes used, more positively, in the early stages of building a pond to tread the chalk and clay to make it non-porous. The name of a pond near Alton Barnes, Oxen Mere, dating from AD 825, suggests that this method may have been followed there and it is possible too that this same method may

89 She was buried in the churchyard.

90 Edward Martin, *Dew Ponds: History, Observation and Experiment*, Laurie, 1914 . See Mary Delorme, *Curious Wiltshire*, Ex Libris Press, 1985, p. 81.

91 Mr Baker was an uncle of Ken Taylor. Information given to the author by Greta Taylor, the widow of Ken Taylor, on 19 June 2004.

92 Described by Dr Williams Freeman in 1915 in his 'Introduction to Field Archaeology'. See *The Wiltshire Archaeological Magazine*.

have been used by Bronze and Iron Age people locally to ensure water supplies for their hill forts.

THE SHEEP WASH

Another, totally different, aspect of sheep rearing was dipping to clean the fleeces. The two ponds now owned by Michael Gaiger were probably originally made to enable this, as the Hawkswell spring itself would not have produced a sufficient head of water for the operation. Witnesses still alive in the 1950s had inherited the understanding that the sluice on the upper pond was operated by the 'Tonkin' – two large posts with a heavy beam across, to which a heavy mechanism to open and close the sluice was attached. The 'bung' for the lower pond was a huge wooden block with a large ring and a long iron crook was kept at Glebe Farm for fishing for the ring from a punt. In the 1860s and 1870s the ponds were 100 feet wide and many hundreds of yards long,[93] much larger than they were in the 1950s, when timber trees grew where there had once been a sheet of water.[94]

The sheep wash was, according to these same accounts, below the lower pond – a very solid masonry erection some 12 foot x 10 foot. Inside were two large wooden tubs, in which the sheep were washed individually. Men, in waterproof clothing and large 'hood hats', held the sheep's head above water as they twisted the animal over and over until it was clean – two strong spouts of water filling the chamber under pressure from the upstream ponds. Each animal was then allowed to swim over to the ramp leading out, assisted sometimes by the shepherd's crook, to dry as best it could.[95]

It has been suggested that the Cotswold method, of throwing the sheep backwards into the pool and then forcing it to swim under a boom before climbing out, might also have been followed in Little Cheverell.[96] It is true that the pool which forms within the brick structure is deep enough for this to have been a possibility; however, the

93 This is confirmed by the 1722 map drawn by John Edgar for Sir Edward des Bouverie.

94 'Little Cheverell Village History'.

95 Photographs testify to this method having been used in the nearby village of Bratton.

96 'Cheverell Parva 19th Century Sheep Washing Pool', pamphlet.

earlier eyewitness accounts of those who saw how the sheep washing was actually done in the village cannot easily be dismissed.

Whatever the procedure, dipping was done only a short time before shearing, although later practice was for sheep to be shorn first and wool washed afterwards. In that earlier epoch no chemicals were used, as they were later, and the washing was done in the fresh water of the chalk stream.

The sheep wash, which is believed to date – in the form in which it was last used – from the nineteenth century, was restored in 2003 and 2004 through the efforts of the Village Hall Committee with grants from the Heritage Lottery Fund, the Countryside Agency and Nationwide. Clearing the site of vegetation was done by a team of ten village volunteers with three from the British Trust for Conservation Volunteers (BCTV) and this restored village feature was formally opened by a representative of Nationwide in June 2004 in the presence of the Lord Lieutenant, Lieutenant General Sir Maurice Johnston, KCB, after a speech by the Chairman of the Parish Council, Helena Warnock.

WOOL AND THE CLOTH TRADE

'In the times of Ancient Britons, Romans, and Saxons and ever since, the spare moments of the housewife, her maids and daughters had been devoted to spinning – the supposed occupation of our mother Eve.' So wrote the historian G. M. Trevelyan. He went on: 'the cloth trade held its place as incomparably the most important English industry, till the far-distant day when coal was wedded to iron. For centuries it occupied men's daily thought in town and village, second only to agriculture; our literature and common speech acquired many phrases and metaphors borrowed from the manufacture of cloth – such as "threads of discourse", "web of life", "homespun", "tease" and "spin a yarn".' Even now unmarried women are still described as 'spinsters' when their Banns of Marriage are published in Church of England churches and, similarly, the use of the word 'distaff', which stems from the ancient method of spinning cloth, originally meant a staff about three feet long with a cleft in it, on which wool or flax was wound. As this task was done in the home by women, the word came to mean women's work – when it was still permissible to talk in such terms – and, by extension, female authority or influence.

Weaving like spinning was also a home industry, done in the cottages and giving rise to such names as Webb, Webber and Weaver. Very young children were therefore involved, before they were old enough to be apprenticed, not only in spinning but also weaving for the cloth industry. This prompted Daniel Defoe to note that 'there was not a child in the town [Taunton in Somerset] or in the villages round it of above five years old but, if it was neglected by its parents and untaught, could earn its bread.' After the coming of steam power in the nineteenth century, however, and the invention of Hargreaves's 'spinning jenny' and Crompton's 'mule', weavers and spinners alike were inevitably drawn into the factories.

From the fourteenth to the eighteenth and nineteenth centuries, the wool trade – particularly in broadcloth 'whites' – was vitally important to both the national and local economies and many fine houses were built in the vicinity on its profits. G. M. Trevelyan wrote: 'The enormous advantage that England had over other countries as a feeder of sheep and a producer of the best wool gave her the opportunity to win the command of the world's cloth market, as she had long commanded the European market for raw wool.'

Peasants of ordinary manors dealt in wool, often owning between them more sheep than those on the lord of the manor's demesne, and this could well have applied in Little Cheverell.[97] Certainly some of the wool from Little Cheverell would have found its way to Trowbridge, which was a renowned woollen-cloth-making town from at least the twelfth century, boasting an individual mark highly regarded both in the warehouses of Manchester and London and among the tailors of Savile Row.

Some idea of how wool and cloth from Little Cheverell may have reached the wider markets in the sixteenth century is given by the detailed records of a Tudor merchant called Thomas Kytson, a freeman of the Mercers Company and a member of the Merchant Adventurers Company. As it is rare for such records to have survived, his books – which he kept in a mixture of abbreviated French, Latin and English – are of especial interest.

Wiltshire 'clothmen' came second only to their Somerset neighbours in supplying Kytson with 'white' broadcloth which was England's main export in the Tudor period. Kytson bought great quantities from as

97 G. M. Trevelyan, *English Social History,* p. 7. (Reprint Society Edition, 1948.)

many as seventy 'clothmen' – from places all over the county, some close to Little Cheverell including Westbury, Devizes, Keevil, Melksham, Trowbridge, Steeple Ashton, Calne, Bromham, Edington and Erlestoke.[98] For instance in 1529 he bought from John Cooper of Edington 'whites' for £25.6s.8d the pack – £2.10s.8d each and one 'fyn whit' at £3.6s.8d – and on 29 May 1536 he bought from John Norington of Devizes 42 whites at about £30 the pack. The packs were normally of ten lengths and the length of a single broadcloth was 25 yards.

Kytson's records detail the names of the 'clothmen' and women, the carriers, the ships' masters and the purchasers, but unfortunately the names of the actual sheep farmers, spinners and weavers, on whose labour the whole cloth trade depended, are unknown. Obviously a village as small as Little Cheverell can only have been a minor player in the wool trade. There can, however, be little doubt that it was important for the farmers, spinners and weavers in the village and that their 'whites' were sold to some neighbouring 'clothman' such as Richard Cross of Erlestoke, John Norington of Devizes or John Duffell of Westbury.

English woollen cloth reached markets as far distant as Morocco and Mali in great quantities but export to the Continent, particularly for the looms of Flanders and Italy, was particularly lucrative. Unfinished English 'whites' were converted in Antwerp, which at that time had a virtual monopoly of this type of business, to the fully-dressed and dyed cloth sought by the European middle classes. No less than 1,348 cloth finishers and journeymen were involved and Kytson's share of this business being considerable, he maintained a house staffed with servants in Antwerp. Trading went on throughout the year and convoys of ships set out from London, laden also with tin, lead and leather, to catch the four important seasonal marts in Flanders – at Easter, Pentecost, St Bavo's Fair at the time of the feast of the Assumption in August and the Cold Mart commencing on the Thursday before All Hallow's Eve on 31 October.

OTHER ASPECTS OF THE LOCAL ECONOMY: MILLS

A malt house and mill operated from Bridge House from the early part of the eighteenth century until it became defunct for some reason at an

98 'Thomas Kytson and Wiltshire Clothmen 1529–1539', *The Wiltshire Archaeological and Natural History Magazine*, vol. 97, 2004, pp. 35–62.

unknown date between 1860 and 1914. After that it became a dwelling house, although there are traces of its former use in Bridge House itself and in Pillar Box Cottage next door. The malt mill was mentioned in a lease from Butcher to Axford in 1749 and manorial records show Thomas Axford as tenant maltster there in 1768.

A mill – presumably Cheverell mill, a water mill for grinding flour – is recorded in the 1086 Domesday entry for Little Cheverell, although it refers, curiously, to half a mill for taxation purposes, possibly because the other half of the assessment was attributable to Great Cheverell. This mill is located on the boundary between the two parishes. Although it probably remained in continuous operation from the eleventh century onwards, there is no record to prove it until 1439 when the miller was 'amerced'[99] for taking excessive toll. From then on, however, it seems to have run continuously until 1914. Conveyed with the manor in 1468, it was held 'customarily' of the manor in the sixteenth and seventeenth centuries and new millstones were installed around 1513 – when the miller was still required to give preference to the lord's tenants. In 1609 the mill was valued at £18 a year. Although the house and mill itself were substantially rebuilt in 1824, as witness an inscription bearing this date on the outside, its greater age is revealed by some late-sixteenth-century woodwork and seventeenth-century stonework. The mill had an 'overshot wheel' fourteen feet in diameter and was driven, as it always had been, by the Hawkswell stream.[100] The last miller was Abraham Whiting, who was also a baker, supplying his bread to both Cheverells.

BRICKWORKS

Bricks were made in Little Cheverell for well over a hundred years, although the exact date at which the business was founded is unclear. Already, however, by 1802 the inclosure award shows that James Bolter, who was born in 1762 and died in 1833, had a brickworks on a twenty-acre field of glebe land held on lease from the rector. Throughout the nineteenth century the Bolter family manufactured bricks and all five of James Bolter's sons were engaged in the undertaking, at least for some time. On their father's death his son, Isaac,

99 Fined.
100 *Victoria County History*, vol. X, p. 58.

was the main beneficiary of his father's will and inherited the business. Prospering as brickmaker, he termed himself 'Master Brickmaker employing six men' in the 1861 census. Prospering equally as a farmer, he used land adjacent to the brickworks to which he had title to build Furze Hill Farm in about 1845[101] and became a significant figure in the village.

On Isaac Bolter's death in 1865 the business and property was inherited by his only surviving son, Abraham, who married his brother Jonah's widow Sarah Jane. Abraham ran the brickworks until his death in 1890 at the age of fifty-five, when his wife took it over. Like his father he also became involved in farming but on a wider scale and from 1879 he and his family lived, as we have seen, at Glebe Farm House. Although Abraham and Sarah Jane had seven sons (Isaac, Abraham, James, William, Thomas, Benjamin and Joseph) and two daughters (Elizabeth and Annie), none of them took over the brickworks. In 1895, therefore, Sarah Jane sold it, with Furze Hill Farm, to Charles Turner under whom it continued to prosper.

Most of the bricks used locally in the nineteenth and early part of the twentieth centuries would have come from this brickworks and Charles Turner's pride that all the bricks for Hawkswell House came from his works has already been mentioned. In 1916 the brickyard and field were leased out by the rector for £27 a year, with royalties if more than 350,000 bricks were made in a year. The last year in which the brickworks are recorded as a business was 1928,[102] although it probably actually closed in the early 1930s.[103]

Although a machine was invented by Cook and Cunningham in 1839 which turned out 18,000 bricks in ten hours, it is not clear whether it was ever used in Little Cheverell. It is certain, however, that for a long time the bricks were made by manual labour. The clay, taken out of the ground on the site itself in the autumn, was exposed to the rains and frosts of winter and this, with the addition of some sand, had the effect of making it tougher and more plastic. After the winter the clay was first kneaded by the feet of workers or cattle, although a steam engine was used in the early twentieth century to break the clay up. After that it was put into wooden moulds and,

101 Finally knocked down in the 1970s.
102 Gillman's *Devizes Almanack*.
103 *Victoria County History*.

when dry, the bricks were piled in the kiln and baked for between forty and sixty hours.

THE KING'S PEACE AND JUSTICE

The institutions which most affected the lives of ordinary people over the ages were the parish, centred on the church, and the manor. The question, however, of how Little Cheverell fitted into the wider national pattern of justice and administration is none the less pertinent. Law and order at village level was for centuries the responsibility of 'tithingmen', who exercised a form of local community policing, but they fitted into a wider system explained below. As late as the eighteenth century they still retained some responsibilities, including returning jurymen for Quarter Sessions.[104]

THE MANORIAL COURT'S JURISDICTION OVER SMALL OFFENCES

The lord of the manor and his court were closest to the villagers of Little Cheverell and there were in fact two manorial courts – the Court Baron and the Court Leet. As we have seen, the Court Baron dealt mainly with local land dealings such as changes of tenant under the copyhold customary tenure but the Court Leet – over which the lord of the manor's steward presided in the capacity of a judge – had a limited jurisdiction over small offences where immediate redress was required. For instance, in 1533 a Little Cheverell woman was brought before the manorial court for being a 'common gossip' and in 1537 a man was prosecuted for being a poacher unlawfully keeping hunting dogs. It is not clear when the last hearing of the Court Leet took place but the rector, in response to questions put to him for the 'Collection for the Parochial Histories of Wilts' in the 1860s, wrote: 'Courts Leet were formerly held but have ceased to be so for many years.'

Above the manor there were county and national institutions with wider powers and at the apex in the county stood the High Sheriff.

104 They had to be sworn in by a JP to perform this role. Constables too had to be sworn to return jurymen. *The Notebook of William Hunt 1744–1749*, ed. Elizabeth Critall, published by The Wiltshire Record Society 1982 (repr. 1987).

The powers of the High Sheriff in the county were unparalleled until the appointment of Lords Lieutenant by King Henry VIII and even then the Sheriff still took local precedence over the Lord Lieutenant until 1904. Over the centuries many of the High Sheriff's original powers, including the jurisdiction of the Sheriff's court, were gradually transferred to others, including the Royal Courts, the judges on Assize and justices of the peace, who sat at quarter and petty sessions. This process prompted the great constitutional lawyer Frederick William Maitland (1850–1906) to comment: 'The whole history of English justice and police might be brought under this rubric, "The Decline and Fall of the Sheriff".'[105] Later the High Sheriff's main functions came gradually to be responsibility for the judges' arrangements in the county and the execution and return of High Court writs. Even this responsibility for writs was – quickly though controversially – removed by legislation in the early years of the twenty-first century by the government of Mr Tony Blair's period as prime minister.

In the Sheriff's heyday, however, from the tenth to the fifteenth centuries, the judicial, executive and administrative powers he could exercise were enormous. From the time when in AD 900 Gawdulf was recorded as holding the office of High Sheriff in Wiltshire, most aspects of justice were in the Sheriff's hands and he was responsible for supervising the system of communal responsibility for crime and for maintaining the peace – especially in the first centuries after the Norman Conquest. He thus, albeit only for a year at a time lest he should grow too powerful, presided over the county, which was divided into hundreds, in every sense.

Surprisingly perhaps, for so small a village, Little Cheverell produced no less than six High Sheriffs over the last thousand years: Sir Alexander Cheverell, 1308 and 1309; Thomas Long, 1653; John Long, 1668; Colonel Robert Awdry, 1928; Admiral John Luce, CB, 1930; Lady Hawley, 1998.

Of these Alexander Cheverell lived in the Manor House, described above, to the south of the church. It is not clear where the Longs lived when they held the demesne farm, but tree planting and an avenue of trees suggest that they may have lived in a house – perhaps later burnt

105 Holdsworth, *A History of English Law*, Methuen and Co Ltd , 5th edition 1931, p. 66.

down[106] – roughly where Hawkswell House now stands. On the other hand there is no sign of such a house on the 1722 map produced by John Edgar for Sir Edward des Bouverie. As this was immediately after the last member of the Long family lived in the village, this theory must be dubious, especially as that map does show a house larger in size than any other in the village, lying to the east of Manor Farm House in what is now a paddock. That seems to provide a more plausible answer to the conundrum of where the Longs lived. Although they did not hold the manor, the Longs were an old and prominent family in Wiltshire and other members of this family held the Mill estate in Great Cheverell.

Robert Awdry lived at Hawkswell House and John Luce and Ruth Hawley[107] at Little Cheverell House during their respective shrieval years.

HUNDREDS

It was King Alfred the Great, who divided the counties into 'hundreds', which were originally groups of 100 free families or possibly geographical units of 100 'hides'. Within the 'hundred' everyone was brought into a 'tithing' of ten men and their families, presided over by a 'tithing man'. They were thus 'knit together in a society – all being bound to the King for their peaceable and good behaviour'.[108] This communal responsibility was extended by the Norman system of frankpledge, which made every member of a tithing group responsible as a compulsory pledge – or 'borh' in Saxon – for the others in it and, in the event of crime, for the production of the person accused. Though now of only historical interest, the 'hundred' remained the unit of local administration in the country until the development of other forms of local government in the nineteenth century.

106 'Little Cheverell Village History'.

107 By 2006 Wiltshire had only had four lady High Sheriffs. The first was Ela, Countess of Salisbury, who was daughter of the second Earl of Salisbury and, when her husband the third Earl died, she followed him as Sheriff in 1228, 1229 and 1231 to 1235. The second was Mrs (Anna) Grange from 1994 to 1995 and third Lady (Ruth) Hawley from 1998 to 1999. Mrs (Geraldine) Wimble became High Sheriff in 2006.

108 Jowitt, *The Dictionary of English Law*, Sweet and Maxwell, 1959.

Little Cheverell, like its sister village Great Cheverell, was in the Swanborough hundred. Curiously Swanborough – mentioned as 'Swana beorh' in AD 987 – was never a village but merely the name of an ancient meeting place at the Tump (a word meaning a bowl barrow, a barrow, mound or clump of trees), in the parish of Manningford Abbots near the boundary with Wilcot. Equally curiously, both Little and Great Cheverell were situated in a sort of 'island' falling under Swanborough jurisdiction surrounded by the Potterne and Cannings hundred on the east; Heytesbury hundred to the south; and Melksham to the west. Swanborough was a royal hundred until 1649 – the Civil War period – and the 'fee' or overall freehold was 'in the Crown and the Government in the Sheriff and his Officers'.[109] The 'fee' then passed into the hands of William Pitt, Earl of Chatham, prime minister 1756–60, from whom William Bouverie, first Earl of Radnor, bought it in 1767.[110]

Little Cheverell, like other villages, was in earlier times expected to send a 'tithingman' to attend the hundred court and also higher courts such as the Sheriff's tourn. The court of the Sheriff, who could impose suitable penalties as long as he had jurisdiction, was part of the tourn proceedings and, as he was a royal deputy, it had the status – until the system was later changed – of a 'court of record', the recorded proceedings of which could not be called in to question.[111]

The Sheriff[112] held two annual courts for the tourn in the Swanborough hundred and it became traditional for the Lady Day court to be held at Foxley Corner[113] near Urchfont, a mile to the east of the village at the meeting of two roads. The other meeting, at Michaelmas, was held at Swanborough Tump. By the seventeenth century, however, it had become customary to adjourn the meeting to more agreeable surroundings – the Rose and Crown in Woodborough for the Swanborough meeting and the Wheat Sheaf in Urchfont for the Foxley Corner meeting.

109 Cox's *Wiltshire 1731*, p. 130.
110 Pitt the Elder.
111 Courts of record were 'courts whose judicial acts and proceedings are enrolled for a perpetual memorial and testimony, which rolls are called the records of the court, and are of such high and pre-eminent authority that their truth is not to be called into question'. Jowitt, *The Dictionary of English Law*.
112 The office came later to be known as High Sheriff.
113 Also known as 'Foxley Burch' or 'Foxley Bush'.

Tithing men from Little Cheverell would over the years no doubt have attended many tourns and hundred courts. However, the record of the Sheriff's tourn for the Swanborough hundred held 'on Wednesday next after the feasts of Saints Tiberius and Valerian' on 14 April1439,[114] at which a tithing man from Little Cheverell was certainly present, is perhaps typical and it gives some idea of the sort of business transacted. The official account – a formal document in Latin[115] – rendered to King Henry VI,[116] includes the following entry relevant to the village:

> Cheverell Parva ...paid 4 shillings. John Norton and Matthew de Aune [or Anne] fined 6 pennies each for breaking the assize of beer. Also for selling beer in false measure [per siphos et discos false mensure]. The Tithing saith it hath not the said 'siphos'. John Norton, miller, fined for over toll.

This would have followed from the tithing men's report and, as a body, it seems that they were dissatisfied with the quality of the local beer.

The fining of a miller was extremely common in those days and many of the entries for other parishes, including Cheverell Magna – where John Russell was accused of the entirely different fault of allowing the 'King's Highway to be overflowed' – also refer to such a case.[117] The twelve jurymen for the hundred, whose function was quite different from that of a modern jury, were in this case 'John Stampford and his fellows'. They confirmed all the 'presentments' made to the tourn, in some cases making a recommendation on who should right the wrong.

The cases from other parishes in the hundred and elsewhere brought to the Swanborough tourn in 1439 illustrate the sort of problems and

114 *The Wiltshire Archaeological and Natural History Magazine*, no. XXXVIII, vol. XIII, May 1872.

115 Latin and French were the languages used in the courts and a number of legal terms still used, or used until relatively recently, have their origin in Norman French – for example 'mortgage', 'Assizes' and 'femme sole', 'en ventre sa mere' and 'cestui que trust'.

116 Sometimes called 'Tour'.

117 The original document was found in the collection of the Marquess of Bath and a detailed account of it by the Revd Canon J. E. Jackson is published in *The Wiltshire Archaeological and Natural History Magazine*, no. XXXVIII, vol. XIII of May 1872. I am grateful to Mr Bryan Coupe of Great Cheverell for drawing my attention to this.

remedies which might have been ordered for Little Cheverell on other occasions. A tithing might be ordered to repair the highway or a bridge – by locally recruited and unpaid labour – or fined for non-compliance. Nicholas Tyler at Sterte was ordered, for instance, to scour his ditches to prevent overflow on to the highway and Philip Manyng, a butcher of Charlton who sold bad meat, was punished.

In some 1439 cases the 'presentment' of tithingmen led to arrests and court action. In Bereford in the hundred of Kyngbridge John Haytor was fined because his 'dung heap encroaches on the highway' and his person was 'attached' – that is, he was arrested – because 'he harbours whores and talebearers day and night to the common nuisance of the neighbourhood'. Similarly in the parish of Brudecombe in the Brench and Droll hundred it was presented that 'Lettice, wife of Godefelowe, is a common brawler' and that 'Joan, wife of John Wattys, is a common thief'. Both were ordered to be arrested and were no doubt tried by the court. In the parish of Stapull in the hundred of Doneworth, Nicholas Nedel was presented as 'a nightwalker and disturber of the peace'. In some cases the accused was placed 'at the mercy of the court' and, at such trials, the facts were established by subjective local knowledge rather than objective evidence given in court in the modern manner.

It was not long after the 1439 Sheriffs' tourn that, in 1461, the power of Sheriffs to arrest people or impose fines or amercements was removed. After that they had to transmit indictments to the justices of the peace for action and thus the more modern system of administering justice began and the Sheriff's major functions began to shrink in the manner described by Maitland.

SERIOUS CRIME AND THE ASSIZES

Onerous responsibilities rested from an early date on the tithing man in respect of serious crime. In 1166 the Assize of Clarendon in the reign of King Henry II (1154–89) – held at the Royal Palace of that name near Alderbury in Wiltshire south west of Salisbury – obliged tithing men to inform the Sheriff or one of the king's judges 'if in their hundred or township there be any man who is accused or suspected of being a robber, murderer or thief or any man who is a receiver of robbers, murderers, or thieves'.[118] In practice presentments about such crimes,

118 Holdsworth, *A History of English Law*, vol. 1, p. 77.

together with others affecting the maintenance of order and good government in their area, came to be made to a jury of twelve free men of the hundred. This was later known as the grand jury and is to be clearly distinguished from that impanelled to try the case, which was known as the petty jury. If they accepted the presentment, they passed it to the Sheriff, who sent the case to the itinerant King's Justices on Assize. The grand jury, which made a decision on whether there was a prima facie case against the accused, remained an integral part of the judicial system until 1933[119] – and so it remains in the United States, where the early colonies followed the English Common Law.

THE WILTON ASSIZE OF 1281

Assizes, presided over by the king's judges, were held from the twelfth century onwards and civil cases, as well as serious criminal offences, were tried. The assize held at Wilton in 1281 is of especial interest to the village, as John de Cheverell, the lord of the manor, was a plaintiff in a case heard there. One John Bever had, on returning from military service abroad, probably in France, obtained possession of a free tenement in Erlestoke previously held by his father Richard. This he sold to John de Cheverell, who claimed that he had been 'disseised' of it because, without any court order, John Bever's younger brother and others had seized it. John de Cheverell therefore sought to obtain 'seisin', a term of Anglo-Norman law meaning possession. The jurors were at this period, as we have seen, local witnesses to events, unlike modern juries and they confirmed the correctness of John de Cheverell's statement of claim. The court accordingly found in his favour and ordered that he should recover his 'seisin', while the younger Bever and his collaborators were 'attached' and ordered to pay him damages of 40 pence.

This, however, was not John de Cheverell's only cause at the Wilton Assize. He also brought an action of 'nouvel disseisin' against the lord of the manor of Erlestoke and two others – probably officials of the manorial court such as the hayward or a 'teller' – for dispossessing him

119 With some exceptions the grand jury was abolished by the Administration of Justice (Miscellaneous Provisions) Act 1933 and finally ended by the Criminal Justice Act 1948. The trial jury on the other hand – originally known as the petty jury – has survived, although its origins and working were very far from and different from the modern jury system.

of the right of common pasture on 200 acres of common for his 'horses, cattle and swine without number'. This case, however, he lost because the evidence of the manor's bailiff, confirmed by the jury, proved that John de Cheverell owned no land in Erlestoke other than the land acquired from John Bever and that neither John Bever nor his father had enjoyed any rights of common pasture as 'appurtenances' of that particular holding. The court accordingly ordered John de Cheverell to pay a fine for a false claim and mulcted[120] his sureties in the sum of £5.

At this point the story begins to resemble a Shakespearean tragedy. John Bever, the vendor, apparently had a reputation as a man of 'a troublesome disposition' and had earlier been found guilty of killing William de la Ford, although he was pardoned by King Henry III following the intercession of his son, Prince Edmund. On the death of King Henry this pardon was confirmed by King Edward I, who succeeded his father, but, shortly after the assize, John Bever was found hanged. John de Cheverell also died at nearly the same time, though King Edward issued instructions to the Sheriff of Wiltshire to deliver possession of the Erlstoke land to Alexander de Cheverell, John's son and his successor as lord of the manor of Little Cheverell.

These cases help to illustrate the relationship between the lord of the manor, the assize court, the Sheriff of the county and the King himself. At a more humble level there are numerous references in the rolls of this assize to 'free tenants' of the manor and to the 'villeins' or customary tenants redeeming part of the service owed to the lord by a money payment. This indicates clearly that the relationship between the lord of the manor and the 'villeins' at Erlestoke was already changing in the thirteenth century. Other indications are that the lord's bailiff there was able to employ labourers instead of the former villein's obligation to work on the demesne lands and that the villeins' customary service, of carrying salt and meat to the lord's larder, was commuted for a gift (called a lardarium) to the lord on the feast of St Dionysius.[121]

LATER ASSIZES AND QUARTER SESSIONS

The forum for the trial of serious criminal cases came over the years to be – according to the seriousness of the offence – either the assizes or

120 Mulcted is an old legal term meaning fined.

121 Article by John Watson Taylor in *The Wiltshire Archaeological and Natural History Magazine*, vol. XXXIV, p. 79.

quarter sessions. The justices of the peace met four times a year for quarter sessions from 1363 onwards and the assizes, held periodically, were presided over by judges of the High Court. Both these courts often sat in Devizes from the fourteenth century onwards in various premises.

Among eighteenth-century criminal cases involving Little Cheverell people presented to the grand jury at quarter session in Devizes, two have come to light. In 1728 a complaint was lodged against Jonathan Hiscock by his wife Edith and signed by four tithingmen, including Hew Skylling, Jno Wadman and H. Townsend Jun. Hiscock was accused of a very serious assault and battery on his wife, which would certainly have aroused the sympathy and anger of the general public, as well as feminists, in later generations. The presentment read:

> Edith, wife of Jonathan Hiscock of Cheverell Parva, saith that about a fortnight ago Jonathan her husband did bind and very much abuse her by tying her hands for the space of five or six hours and then threw her in some water. Afterwards he took her into ye house with all her wett dirty clothes about her and did sundry times put stinging nettles under her shift and tyed her to ye frame of ye tableboard in ye said house and about two or three dayes after he did take a hempen halter and hang her by the neck to ye lamme[122] of ye house until she was almost dead, and at ye same time put stinging nettles under her shift to see if she was really dead or no, which was done by the persuation of William Blake of Cheverell Parva, yeoman, who had sundry times before spoke to ye said Jonathan to stopp her breath that he might hear no more of ye said Edith.

No doubt Jonathan Hiscock received condign punishment, but unfortunately the author has not yet been able to find the result of the trial.

The other case involved William Glass, who in 1742 was indicted by a grand jury on a charge of pound breach – a very serious offence at that time. The indictment read:

> The Jury of our Lord the King upon their oath present that there is, and from the time whereof the memory of man is not to the contrary was, a common pound in Little Cheverell ... and that the 2nd day of October in the 16th year of the reign of our Sovereign

122 Beam.

> Lord George II, by the Grace of God etc, one cow the property of William Glass of Little Cheverell, gardener, was lawfully impounded and detained in the pound aforesaid for damage done in the lands of Thomas Axford of Little Cheverell, and that the said William Glass the third day of October in the aforesaid with force and arms[123] and so forth at Little Cheverell the common pound did break and take the said cow so impounded and detained out of the pound took and led away to the great damage of the said T. Axford and against the peace of the said King his crown and dignity.

Some of today's farmers can perhaps count themselves fortunate that the common pound no longer survives!

In 1835 a new and prestigious Court House designed by Thomas Wyatt was built of Bath stone in Devizes in classical Palladian style. Built by public subscription, it became, from then on, the venue not only for the assizes and quarter sessions but also petty sessions – the local magistrates' court, where lesser cases were dealt with. The assize judges' accommodation too was improved when in 1869 the town council acquired the former King's Arms, opposite the court in Northgate Street, for the judges' lodgings. The formal opening in the presence of the High Sheriff of each session of the assizes – principally 'Nisi Prius', 'Oyer and Terminer'[124] and 'General Gaol Delivery' – used always to be marked by a colourful procession to the Court House. This carried on until 1972, when the assizes and quarter sessions were replaced by a single crown court by virtue of the Courts Act 1971. The administration of justice for local people was moved one stage further away when, in 2005, the magistrates' court in Devizes was closed for regular sittings and cases formerly heard there transferred to the Chippenham venue.

As regards penalties, the law and practice inclined towards greater leniency throughout the nineteenth and twentieth centuries and the death penalty for murder, finally abolished in 1965, was replaced with a mandatory life sentence. In earlier generations local people saw for themselves the consequences of a conviction for murder and, as relatively recently as 1860, executions were carried out publicly in Devizes. When, for instance, Rebecca Smith was hanged in 1849 for the murder

123 'Vi et armis'.
124 Norman French for to 'hear and determine' – civil actions.

of her infant child with rat poison, the event was watched by a crowd estimated at 30,000, amongst whom there would surely have been some from Little Cheverell.

JUSTICES, PETTY CRIME AND BREACHES OF THE PEACE

Sometimes petty crimes and complaints were dealt with even closer home than Devizes by a justice of the peace. Some illustrations of this are given in *The Justicing Notebook of William Hunt 1744–1749*.[125] He was first named as a JP in the commission of the peace for Wiltshire on 29 July 1743 at the age of forty-seven and the 'division' to which he was assigned embraced the hundred of Swanborough, in which Little Cheverell lies, as well as the hundreds of Potterne and Cannings.

William Hunt was the eldest son of Thomas Hunt of West Lavington and Mary Grubbe, daughter of an old family of Eastwell at Potterne. Educated at Trinity College, Oxford and the Middle Temple, he was well qualified for the magistracy and, in this capacity, attended quarter sessions not only at Devizes but also at Marlborough, Calne, Warminster and Salisbury. Exercising delegated or statutory petty sessions powers, he also often sat with one other magistrate or alone very locally – at the Horse and Jockey[126] in West Lavington or the Dragon or the Bell at Market Lavington.

Typical petty sessions cases, in which he was involved, included thefts, profane swearing, breaches of the Lord's Day, such as selling liquor or tippling during the hours of divine service, vagabonds, people staying in places other than their place of legal settlement, and the issue of passes to those lawfully passing through the county. Sometimes too William Hunt sat with one or two commissioners, who were not JPs, for special sessions for land and window taxes, and he often sat with the Revd John Shergold, rector of Little Cheverell, as a commissioner. Other special sessions included 'brewster sessions' for the licensing of alehouses; sessions for highways, at which appointments of surveyors were made and their presentments on the state of roads received; and sessions to deal with recalcitrant overseers, unwilling to disgorge their accounts.

125 Edited by Elizabeth Critall and published by the Wiltshire Record Society 1982.
126 Now a private house, the home of Colonel John and Ann Janes.

As a single magistrate, he swore in tithingmen and constables, whose duties included making a return of those qualified to sit as jurymen at quarter sessions. He was a magistrate when it was necessary to bring the Army and the Navy up to strength because of Bonnie Prince Charlie's invasion in 1745 and the War of Austrian Succession, which began in 1744 – the last war in which an English king commanded his troops in the field, at the Battle of Dettingen. Hunt was therefore also a recruiting commissioner, whose duties included the swearing in of men for service.

All the Little Cheverell cases he heard were relatively trivial, including a few petty thefts. Four were thefts of wood, two of turnips and one a new spade. It was probably real necessity which drove people to commit such thefts and in earlier centuries the stealing of wood and turnips had been regarded rather lightly. However, by the eighteenth century these offences had come to be dealt with formally as crimes. William Hunt, appreciating this, appears to have understood people's real circumstances and he exercised his duties with considerable humanity, compassion and common sense, settling cases by arbitration if he could.

William Hunt brought the parties to agreement in a number of Little Cheverell wood-stealing cases including those of John Hampton against Edward Hayward and Daniel Smith Junior and of Timothy Somner against Nicholas Crouch. In the case, however, of the widow Mary Alexander against James Boulter, the latter was ordered by Hunt to pay five shillings for the use of the poorer of the parish, to be distributed at the discretion of the complainant. In one case of an alleged theft of turnips, a summons was granted on 18 December 1746 at the complaint of William Dowden of Great Cheverell, a yeoman, against John Mattock, an apprentice of William Hicks, weaver of Little Cheverell, for entering common ground in Little Cheverell and stealing and carrying away a quantity of turnips. It seems that the case was settled by agreement of the parties on their appearance before William Hunt, for they were ordered to pay the cost of the summons.

In another case, James Boulter of Little Cheverell accused John Butcher of Worter (*sic* but probably Worton) of stealing a new spade and was granted a warrant on 8 April 1747. However the complainant later requested that the prosecution should not proceed. On the other hand, William Hunt dismissed as frivolous a complaint by Henry Somner, baker of Great Cheverell, against William Glass, 'gardener', of

Little Cheverell for 'fraudulent delivery of faggots', as no fraud was proved.

Three other Little Cheverell cases were complaints against employers for refusal to pay wages and William Hunt resolved them easily. The yeoman Thomas Axford was twice accused. In the first case, having appeared on summons on 23 July 1745, he agreed to pay husbandry wages due to John Godwin of Great Cheverell. Similarly summoned on 14 January, he agreed to pay wages for husbandry due to Thomas Hayward of Little Cheverell. In the third case William Dowden of Little Cheverell was served with a summons on the complaint of James Smith of Great Cheverell for husbandry wages withheld and the parties reached agreement without appearing before Hunt.

In one 1746 case Robert Howell, a labourer, accused Thomas Bolter of assault but William Hunt reconciled the parties and 'suffered them to agree it'. In a complaint alleging oral abuse, William Slade, a gentleman of Tilshead, was granted a summons on 26 January 1747 against Grace Hampton of Little Cheverell for 'abusing scandalously and illegally ill-treating' him. When, however, she appeared before William Hunt, 'she cleared herself of being the author of the scandal'.

No doubt seemingly righteous anger often aroused people to make formal complaints over relatively petty matters but, after tempers cooled, small issues between neighbours were often fairly easily settled with a little help from a sympathetic local magistrate, already known to them.

The game laws were still strict at this period, even if nothing like as strict as in Norman times. After 1671 the qualification for hunting of any description was possession of land worth at least £100 a year, a considerable acreage. From 1706 only persons so qualified were permitted to keep the dogs, snares etc or other equipment necessary and the statutory penalty for offences against these laws was a fine of £5 or three months' imprisonment. Nevertheless William Hunt, and sometimes indeed the gamekeepers themselves who reported the offence, treated such cases with as much leniency as the law allowed and often the fine imposed was distributed to the poor of the parish.

In one Little Cheverell case of this type William Hunt, on 25 May 1748, convicted William Meek on the oath of James Sainsbury of West Lavington of having in his possession on 22 May ' two wires or engines together with a fish line and hook for destruction of game [presumably hare or rabbits] on Little Cheverell Cliff'. William Meek was sentenced to pay £5 'pursuant to the statute'.Whatever sympathy William Hunt might had for the accused, he had no discretion and was bound to impose the penalty prescribed by the law.

A NINETEENTH-CENTURY CASE OF EXTRA-JUDICIAL VILLAGE JUSTICE

Local justice was also sometimes meted out more summarily and idiosyncratically. A story said to have been 'told and retold' in the village in the second half of the nineteenth century concerned a Mr Young who, coming home very late one Saturday night in a drunken state, proceeded to beat his wife. Six lively boys rapidly found out and decided to avenge her quickly in a manner which may have been a traditional way of ridiculing someone but was more probably novel. Before the Sunday morning service next day, they put up an accusatory notice and at the same time scattered several bags of chaff, taken from a barn belonging to the father of one of them, between the Youngs' cottage and the church gates. The intent, it seems, was to 'chaff'[127] the guilty party and to compare the wife's treatment with chaff produced as a result of threshing . The 'summary sentence' apparently had the desired effect, the wife-beater was contrite and local tradition had it that Mr and Mrs Young 'lived happily ever after'![128]

THOMAS BOULTER – THE LOCAL HIGHWAYMAN

There is a local tradition that the village produced a famous – or infamous – highwayman. It seems, however, that the man who did achieve fame or notoriety in this field was a Thomas Boulter born in 1748, who was the son of the miller at Poulshot. Perhaps some confusion arose because a Thomas, son of Thomas and Mary Boulter of Little Cheverell, who was christened in Little Cheverell Church on 9 November 1740 was a near contemporary and would have been thirty-eight, a plausible age, at the time the highwayman was hanged. In any case it seems inconceivable that Thomas Boulter, the highwayman, did not have some close family connection with the village – with its many Boulters and Bolters.

127 Usage of the word in this sense is described in the Oxford English Dictionary as 'somewhat vulgar'!
128 'Little Cheverell Village History'.

Thomas Boulter operated with a man called Thomas Blagdon of West Lavington from Poulshot Mill and 'had a very busy and distinguished career on the highways of England in general and of Salisbury Plain in particular'. He also committed robberies later with one James Caldwell near places as distant as Ripon, Sheffield, Windsor and Gloucester.[129]

Boulter, who 'took to the road' after his father had been sentenced to fourteen years and transportation for stealing a horse at Trowbridge, was described as of striking appearance, with fair hair, a good figure and smart clothes made by a good tailor. He seems to have been referred to locally as 'Dick Turpin', although the real Turpin died at York in 1739 'under tragical circumstances, with the aid of a rope'. Perhaps Boulter did indeed consciously model himself on Turpin and he certainly gained some local reputation for chivalry and generosity. For instance, although he robbed many farmers and wealthy travellers in coaches, he returned a ring to a lady who burst into tears when he was about to deprive her of it, and spared a farmer who claimed the watch, of which Boulter was about to rob him, was 'of sentimental value'.

Boulter, like Dick Turpin, had a beautiful mare called 'Black Bess' which, emulating his father as a horse thief, he stole from Mr Peter Delme's stables at Erlestoke.[130] A so-called 'Turpin's Stone' erected between Keevil and Bulkington commemorates him with the enigmatic inscription:

> Dicq Turpin's dead and gone,
> This stone's set up to think upon.

Whatever Thomas Boulter's connection with the village may have been, Little Cheverell was certainly in an area where 'gentlemen of the road' operated. 'The neighbourhood of Devizes and Salisbury', according to Charles G. Harper,[131] was 'exceptionally favoured with these

129 *Gentlemen of the Road. Thomas Boulter Highwayman of Poulshott.* Booklet produced for Devizes Carnival in 1976 and researched by Bill Underwood.

130 Charles G. Harper, *Half-Hours with the Highwaymen*, vol. II, p. 238. Curiously, however, this author – though attributing the theft to Thomas Boulter – dates it at 1736. It may be a misprint or something requiring further investigation.

131 *Op. cit.*, vol. I, p. 114.

miscellaneous rascals, no doubt because those two places stood at either extreme of what long remained the wild and desolate region including Salisbury Plain, where, although the great roads to Bath and Exeter brought considerable traffic, the houses were few and far between.' In fact, as anyone can still see today, the old 'slow coach' road to Salisbury from Bath meanders over the very southern part of the parish near New Zealand Farm. Some of the roads on the Plain are still clearly defined with a hardcore of flints, and their hedgerows – mainly of hawthorn elder, briar roses, sloes, ash and wayside apples – still adorn the countryside. It is easy to imagine the coach and horses working gently 'up hill and down dale' – and always in some danger.

One of Thomas Boulter's highway robberies probably took place on 24 December 1777 on the Plain not far from Little Cheverell. The victim was Thomas Fowle, whose notice about it is a vivid reminder of the perils of travel at that period:

Highway Robbery

Whereas Thomas Fowle in the County of Wilts was attacked on Monday afternoon on the Devizes Plain near the 11 Mile Stone, by two Highwaymen who robbed him of five guineas and a half and his watch.

The two men were well-mounted on dark brown horses, one of the horses had both hinder hocks white, they both had surcoats on and appeared to be lusty men. He who robbed Mr Fowle was about five feet 10 inches high and was booted and spurred. Whoever will give notice so as one or more of the above highwaymen may be apprehended shall on conviction receive five guineas reward over and above the £40 allowed by Act of Parliament, to be paid by me.

24 December 1777
Ths. Fowle

The law nonetheless eventually caught up with Boulter and, captured at Bridport while trying to fly to France, he was tried and hanged at Winchester in 1778. A similar fate greeted the group of eighteenth-century highwaymen known as the 'Cherhill Gang', who operated mainly in the region of Marlborough, Calne and Devizes and with which Thomas Boulter could have had some connection, in addition to his other exploits. The bodies of members of this gang, who were tried and hanged in Devizes, were exhibited on a gibbet high on the down between Beckhampton and Cherhill – probably coated in tar, as was then frequent practice, to delay natural decay. Whether Boulter's body was similarly exhibited is not known. It is however not unlikely, for such sights were quite common and a French tourist in 1765 described the gibbets he had seen at the roadside on his way to London: 'there they dangle, dressed from head to foot, and with wigs upon their heads.'

OTHER ROBBERS

Another local reminder of the continuing perils of travel for people in an earlier era is the story behind the erection of the 'Robbers' Stone' on the edge of the parish near Gore Cross and another, connected, stone on Chitterne Down.[132] The inscription reads:

> At this spot Mr Dean of Imber was attacked and robbed by 4 highwaymen in the evening of Oct 21st 1839. After a spirited pursuit of three hours one of the felons, Benjamin Colclough, fell dead on Chitterne Down. Thomas Saunders, George Waters and Richard Harris were eventually captured and were convicted at the ensuing Quarter Sessions at Devizes and transported for the term of fifteen years.
>
> This monument is erected by public subscription as a warning to those who presumptuously think to escape the punishment God has threatened against thieves and robbers.

The inscription on the stone on Chitterne Down reads:

> This monument is to record the awful end of Benjamin Colclough, Highway Robber who fell Dead on this Spot in attempting to escape his pursuers after Robbing Mr Dean of Imber in the Evening of Oct 21st 1839 and was buried at Chitterne without Funeral Rites.
>
> 'Though hand join in hand the wicked shall not be unpunished' Prov. 11.21

The facts were that the robbers pulled Mr Dean off his horse, then two rifled his pockets while a third pressed his nose and his mouth to

132 *News and Views*, March 2005, pp. 13–15 and April, p. 15. Local West Lavington publication.

prevent him giving the alarm and then put his hands over the victim's eyes. They removed a pocket book containing £20 notes from one of his pockets and from another they took a sovereign and a half in gold and £2 in silver. The horse galloped away during the scuffle, but when Mr Dean recovered he followed the men on foot and after fifty or sixty yards met Mr Morgan of Chitterne, who pursued the robbers on horseback, keeping them in his sight. They threatened to shoot anyone who came near them, but Mr Hooper joined the pursuit on horseback and Benjamin Colclough, a stout robber, fell on his back and died. Mr Sainsbury of West Lavington also soon joined in and at last the three remaining robbers were cornered but, armed with large fold sticks, they threatened Mr Sainsbury if he touched them. He, however, held up the large end of his hunting whip and said 'If this is not enough for you, I have a brace of bulldogs (pistols) in my pocket and, if you make the least resistance, I will shoot you dead on the spot.' They then surrendered, the chase having taken three hours.

At the inquest on Colclough, the jury returned a verdict of 'felo de se' – 'the act of one who deliberately puts an end to his own existence or commits an unlawful act the consequence of which is his death'. The jury were so delighted with the action of Mr Morgan in particular that they 'entered into a subscription to buy him a piece of plate'. One wonders whether modern citizens who dealt so effectively with criminals would have received the same commendation or been taken to task for using excessive force.

The three men convicted at the Devizes Quarter Sessions were all transported to Tasmania. Harris and Waters received 'conditional pardons' after thirteen years and eleven years nine months respectively, while Saunders died in prison eleven years after his trial.

These two stones – in a manner unknown today – publicly attribute a criminal's death to God's judgement and similarly a tablet on the market cross[133] memorial in the market square of Devizes commemorates the sudden death of Ruth Pierce of Potterne as warning to others. It reads:

> The Mayor and Corporation of Devizes avail themselves of the stability of this building to transmit to future times the record of an awful event which occurred in this market place in the year 1753 hoping that such record may serve as a salutary warning

133 Erected by Viscount Sidmouth, who was MP for Devizes, in 1814.

against the danger of impiously involving divine vengeance or of calling on the Holy Name of God to conceal devices of falsehood and fraud.

On Thursday the 25th January 1753 Ruth Pierce of Potterne in this county agreed with three other women to buy a sack of wheat in the market, each paying her due proportion towards the same; one of these women in collecting the several quotas of money discovered a deficiency and demanded of Ruth Pierce the sum which was wanting to make good. Ruth Pierce protested that she had paid her share and said she wished she might drop down dead if she had not. She rashly repeated this awful wish when to the consternation and terror of the surrounding multitude she instantly fell down and expired, having the money concealed in her hand.

CONSTABLES AND EARLY POLICING

Systems of communal responsibility gradually changed and constables came to play an increasing role in helping to keep the peace. The origin of the word is 'comes stabuli' and in the eastern Roman empire it signified a superintendent of the imperial stables. However, in England it was used for officers with very different levels of authority. The Lord High Constable was in feudal times a great officer of state, who attended the king at his coronation and military expeditions and, in addition to his jurisdiction in the Court of Chivalry, presided over trials by battle – a form of trial which became obsolescent but was only finally abolished in 1819.[134] The last hereditary Lord High Constable was Edward Strafford, Duke of Buckingham, on whose attainder in 1521 the office was forfeit to the Crown and ceased to exist.

We are, however, concerned rather with the sort of constable at a local level who would have had authority in Little Cheverell. These were of two types: high constables appointed by the hundred court or the court leet with the duty of preserving the peace within their hundred and petty, or parish, constables appointed at petty sessions by the justices. In the Swanborough hundred two constables were appointed – one for the eastern and one for the western side and petty constables operated on a still more local basis. Constables were responsible not only for preserving the peace but also serving summonses, executing the warrants issued

134 W. S. Holdsworth, *A History of English Law*, vol. 1, p. 310.

by the justices and arresting debtors. They also collected money on behalf of the creditor and this function gave rise to such phrases as:

'To pay the constable.'

'Who's to pay the constable?' – i.e. settle the score.

'To outrun the constable' – i.e. to go at too great a pace or to spend more more money than one has.

The jurisdiction of the old constables was largely removed by the County Police Act of 1839 and other Local Government Acts. Regular police forces were then established and the Wiltshire County Police Force was the very first of these – formed in 1839. Its headquarters was in Devizes, as it still is,[135] and Devizes thus became the centre for law and order in the county with the Assize Court, the County Gaol, the County Lunatic Asylum and the headquarters of the Wiltshire Regiment, in which several Little Cheverell men served in the First World War.

THE CHURCH

A church has stood on the present site for over 1,000 years and indeed some form of pre-Christian religious worship might, as elsewhere, have taken place there. The church was for centuries the main focal point for all parish life – in a way that is no longer recognisable – and, from Norman times, Church and State were very closely associated. The lord of the manor had the duty, and privilege, of appointing the rector, who, living close to the people, contributed much, through the records he kept, to present-day knowledge of the village and its past inhabitants.

DEDICATION

In the Middle Ages the church was dedicated to St Nicholas,[136] to whom for long periods more churches in England were dedicated than any other saint or body other than the Virgin Mary and All Saints.[137] St Nicholas, who was born in Patara in about AD 260, was Bishop of Myra on the southern coast of Asiatic Turkey and, famed for his

135 The headquarters moved from the Bath Road opposite the old prison to its present site on the London Road in the 1960s.

136 The Feast of St Nicholas is celebrated on 6 December – particularly in Holland and other European countries.

137 Information given to the author by the Bishop of Salisbury, the Rt Revd David Stancliffe, on 5 December 2004.

generosity and his miracles, became the patron saint of children and of sailors.[138] His cult spread rapidly from Myra to Bari and thence all over Europe (Appendix C). The circumstances of, and date at which, the church came to be known as St Peter's instead of St Nicholas's remain obscure, but it has been dedicated to St Peter since the 1850s.

CHURCH BUILDING

A church certainly stood on the present site in 1291 and the existing bells were installed in the fourteenth century in the tower, where masonry points to a much earlier, Saxon, origin. The chancel and nave were substantially rebuilt in the nineteenth century and all that remains of the earlier church are the square tower, reminiscent with its pitched roof of some French churches, the high Perpendicular arch separating the tower from the nave, the fifteenth-century tracery of the west window, the porch and part of the vestry. The church in its present form is, therefore, a mixture of medieval and nineteenth-century work. Of a chantry chapel, erected by the Cheverell family in 1298 and dedicated to the Virgin Mary, nothing can now be seen, although foundations discovered in 1832 suggest it stood to the north of the chancel.

In the old church a squint – a small opening cut though a chancel arch or wall originally to enable worshippers in an aisle or side chapel to see the elevation of the Host during the Catholic mass – was a feature and it continued in use after the Reformation. The Revd John Fishlake, who may have seen it himself, described it in the 1860s:

> There was in the old Church a very fine hagioscope in the North wall of the Chancel, evidently for the use of the large seat or room attached to the outside of the Chancel, which was the Squire's family seat on the site now occupied by the vestry as built in 1849. The above-mentioned seat was very large and extended a considerable distance into the Northern parts of the Churchyard. The foundation was dug out about 33 years ago and broken to make more room for burials.[139]

138 See further details of St Nicholas in Appendix C.

139 Answers given by the rector in 1862 to the Wilkinson questionnaire on Ecclesiastical and Religious History. Devizes Museum Library. The squint appears to have been removed by the early nineteenth century as J. Buckler's 1807 painting shows no sign of the 'large seat or room' or of the squint.

The original chantry chapel and the squint may therefore have been in nearly the same position at different periods.

NINETEENTH-CENTURY REBUILDING

A watercolour of 1807 by J. Buckler proves that the reconstruction of the building in 1850 – in the time of the Revd John Fishlake as rector[140] – followed both the general shape and style of the earlier church. With Messrs Cundy of London as architects, the work was done by Messrs Bilton and Sainsbury of West Lavington at a cost of £500. The opening morning and evening services were attended by no less than fifteen clergy and a local press report gave detailed coverage to the occasion (Appendix D).

The oak timbers for the roof were cut from Shovel Wood and the carpentry work done in saw pits dug in the wood itself.[141] The oak pews, the pulpit and lectern all date, too, from the middle of the nineteenth century. The steps up to the church were the gift of Mr Walter Pleydell-Bouverie perhaps in the 1880s or 1890s; before that the approach path was described as 'very steep'.[142]

MODERN MAINTENANCE OF THE FABRIC

In 2005 it became evident that the state of the church roof, in particular the chancel, had deteriorated so much that it leaked badly and urgent repair became a necessity. The roof being of stone tiles, specialist roofers were required and an appeal was launched for funds to cover the cost of this and other work on the church fabric. A sum of approximately £30,000 was raised, thanks to the generosity of people in the village, by no means all regular members of the congregation of St Peter's, also of a number of charitable trusts, local businesses (approached by Ruth Hawley on behalf of the Parochial Church Council), the proceeds of a

140 'At Common Law the repair of an ancient church was the obligation of the Rector of the parish, whether spiritual or lay, in the absence of a custom to the contrary, and a lay impropriator in receipt of the rents and profits of the rectory was liable for repair ...' (*Halsbury's Laws of England* , 94th ed., vol. 14, para 1100. Also see Parochial Church Council of Aston Cantlow and Wilmcote with Billesley, Warwickshire v Wallbank (Judgment of 28 March 2000).
141 'Little Cheverell Village History', p. 65.
142 Testimony of an old male villager, collected for the 'History of Little Cheverell'.

concert[143] and of cooking events arranged by Caroline Morison.[144] The work on the chancel part of the roof was completed in the first half of 2005 under the much appreciated supervision of the church architect, Chris Romain, and Gaiger Bros. of Devizes, whose two senior directors, Michael and Vincent Gaiger, live in the village and who generously contributed their expertise. The roof of the tower, completely repaired in 1937, fortunately remained in good condition.

The majority of the windows were replaced with new glass and leading between 2002 and 2004 as a project for the Millennium and the Queen's Golden Jubilee. The cost was met entirely by a combination of a grant from the Wiltshire Historic Churches Trust, the proceeds of an earlier concert in the church given by the Swindon Male Voice Choir, and donations for individual windows from Mr Barny Beddow, the bequest of Mr Freddie Child, Sir Donald and Lady Hawley, Brigadier Peregrine and Mrs Rawlins and available church funds. The windows endowed by donations were marked by a 'lozenge' with the initials – and devices – of the donors; the year; 'dd' to denote donor dedit, and the cross keys of St Peter. The whole project, which was executed by Mr Andrew Turner, a creator of stained glass and expert glazier of Littleton Panell, is commemorated by an inscription on the back north window close to the font, which reads: 'The windows of the Church were restored in 2002–2004 to commemorate the Millennium and Royal Jubilee.'

EAST WINDOW

The stained glass east window was designed by the 'Royal Munich Glass Establishment ... Mayer and Co of 5 Holles Street, Cavendish Square, London W' and installed in 1908 at an estimated cost of £50.[145]

143 It was given by the Swindon Male Voice Choir with Charlotte Eels (soprano), Anna Roberts – wife of Stewart Roberts, Headmaster of Dauntsey's School – (keyboard), Paula Boyagis (flute) and Cobie Smit (guitar).

144 Lady Morison, wife of Sir Thomas Morison, a judge of the High Court. They live at Manor Farm House which they have considerably improved in recent years.

145 Wiltshire County Record Office D1/61/44/36. The original design included the words 'I am the Good Shepherd and I know my sheep' but these words did not appear in the finished window, although the theme is obvious. The 'faculty' for the work was granted by the diocese to the Revd Powley Nicholls as incumbent and Walter Bazell as churchwarden.

It was formally dedicated on Sunday 15 November 1908 by Canon Whiteford, the rural dean, and unveiled by Charles Awdry, then the patron of the living, in the presence of a very full congregation.[146]

The three large panels of this east window are set in the carved stone surrounds. The central figure with a halo is Jesus Christ as the 'Good Shepherd', wearing a robe of rich red, carrying a shepherd's crook, and with one lamb gazing at him, in his arms – a very appropriate theme for a parish dependent on sheep farming. The background is a rural landscape with trees in green, red and yellow and at the Lord's feet are other sheep gazing at him. The left-hand panel contains two figures of saints with halos. They are not as easy to attribute as some figures in other stained glass windows, as they are not given the usual symbols of identity. However, the younger figure is almost certainly St John, 'the disciple whom Jesus loved', also known as St John the Evangelist, though there is some doubt whether he was also the author the Revelation of St John the Divine. There may also be a direct or indirect allusion to St John the Baptist in the figure as he was the first to call Jesus 'the lamb of God'.

The older bearded figure, with a bald head and wearing robes of blue and gold, almost certainly represents St Peter. The sheep look towards Christ and the rural background resembles that of the central panel. The right hand panel contains two figures, without halos but clad in rich robes of green and purple, and they probably represent two Old Testament Prophets who made prophesies about the Messiah. They seem most likely to be Isaiah and either Daniel or Jeremiah. Again the landscape background resembles that of the other two panels and there are sheep – significantly not looking at the two pre-Christian figures but towards the figure of Christ. The other smaller panels of varying sizes contain, starting at the top:

> 'IHS' in calligraphic script. This was originally a contraction for the Greek version of Jesus but has also, variously, been regarded as meaning 'Jesus Hominum Salvator' – Jesus the Saviour of mankind; 'In hac salus' – in this [cross] is safety; 'In hoc signo' – in this sign i.e. the cross with 'vinces' you shall conquer – implied. Another theory suggests that it can represent 'Jesus, Huios, Soter' – the Greek first letters for 'Jesus, Son, Saviour'.

146 Press report of 10 December 1908. Collection, Devizes Museum Library.

Two panels containing winged angels.

Three panels with – left to right – the Greek letter Alpha; a rose wreath in pink and blue, representing the Virgin Mary, the rose without a thorn;[147] and the Greek letter Omega.

Two tiny panels with floral decoration.

Under the window there is a carved wooden reredos depicting the Last Supper, the gift of an earlier rector at the beginning of the twentieth century – apparently the Revd William Powley Nichols.

MEMORIAL TABLETS

There are a number of memorials inside the church:

a) A floor vault stone to the west of the nave leading into the tower, commemorating members of the Axford family, which reads:

Underneath this stone lyeth
The body of Thomas Axford
And of Mary his wife
She died 10 June 1777 aged 66
He died 3 Jan.1778 aged 66
And the body of their Son Thomas who died 11th August
1782 aged 31
In Memory of Mary
Daughter of
Thomas and Mary Axford
Who departed this life
April 1803
Aged 58
Also died the mother of
Jon Axford
Who departed this life
June [obscure]
Aged [obscure]

147 *Inside Churches. A Guide to Church Furnishings*, The National Association of Decorative and Fine Arts Societies, p. 28.

b) A floor vault stone just inside the entrance to the church near the porch, which reads:

Underneath lies buried the body
of Mary, wife of John Shergold MA
Rector of this church
Who died
Sept. 6th 1745
Aged 56 years
And of Mary and Mary
Two of their children
Who died in their infancy

c) Another such stone – badly defaced – seems to read:-

Sacred to the Memory of
John Taylor, Gent.
Late of
Beckenham [Somerset]
Died 21st March 1799
Aged 80 years

d) A white marble plate mounted on a black stone in the chancel on the south wall, reading:

Sacred to the memory
of
The Revd. William Richards
23 years Rector of this parish
Who departed this life July 26th 1823
Aged 63 years
Sincerely lamented by his family and friends
Also
of Katherine his wife
who died December 25th 1835
Aged 64 years

e) A brass plate on the wall inscribed with black and red enamel on the north wall of the chancel, adjoining the pulpit, reading:

Sacred to the memory of
WALTER PLEYDELL-BOUVERIE
Lord of the Manor of this Parish
Son of the Rt. Honble. E. Pleydell-Bouverie
Born July 5th 1848
Died May 20th 1893
And
Edith Pleydell-Bouverie
His wife
Daughter of the Honble. and Revd. J.W. Lascelles
Rector of Goldborough and Canon of York
Born August 5th 1857
Died August 23rd 1902
This tablet was erected
In grateful remembrance by
Parishioners of Little Cheverell
AD 1904

f) A brass plate with the crest of the Royal Navy on the north wall of the nave, reading:

To the most beloved memory of
Admiral John Luce CB
Born at Halcombe Malmesbury 4 Feb 1870
Died at Little Cheverell House 22nd Sept. 1932
High Sheriff of Wiltshire1930 1931
And a Governor of
Dauntsey's School

g) An elaborate memorial high on the north wall of the tower to members of the Alexander family, which reads:

Near this place lieth the body of Edward Alexander who departed this life Jan. 25th 1742 aged 39 years.

Farewell, dear Wife, my life is past
My love to you so long did last
But as for me no sorrow take,
But love my children for my sake.

Also in the same grave lieth the remains of Edward son of

Edward and May Alexander who departed this life May 25th 1782 aged 41

Also Ann wife of Edward Alexander Junior who departed this life Feb. 4th 1822 aged 85 years

Also 4 children of Edward and Ann Alexander who died in infancy

h) Another elaborate memorial on the south wall of the tower opposite the other one to the memory of the Alexander family, which reads:

Sacred to the memory of Mary Alexander who departed his life with truly pious resignation on the 13th July 1790 aged 74 years

Kind angels watch this sleeping dust
Till Jesus come to raise the just
And may thee wake with sweet surprise
An in her Saviour's image rise

Also to the memory of Mary Alexander who departed this life Jan. 22nd aged 60 years

Also to the memory of John Alexander who departed this life June 25 1815 aged 77 years

In 2005 a bench was donated for the churchyard by Mrs Greta Taylor in memory of her husband, Ken, who like his father and uncle were associated with the church throughout their lives. It was blessed by the incumbent, the Revd Harold Stephens, after the 11 a.m. Communion service on Sunday 17 July 2005.

TOMBS AND GRAVES

A number of old and impressive grave memorials in the churchyard include those of the two nineteenth-century rectors, whose joint service spanned nearly eighty-seven years – the Revd John Roles Fishlake, his wife and members of his family, and the Revd William Powley Nichols. A sarcophagus-shaped grave on the left of the path approaching the main church door is that of the Crouch family, erected in the nineteenth century, and there are a number of significant ancient graves, although many of the earlier inscriptions are almost impossible to read.

A High Altar still stood in the church in 1553, although these had earlier been proscribed during the Reformation, and no doubt remained there at least until 1558, when the Catholic Queen Mary was succeeded by her Protestant sister, Queen Elizabeth I.

During the seventeenth century the church went, like the rest of the country, through further turbulent times and the property must have been sequestrated because, on the Restoration of Charles II, Edward Hort successfully petitioned in 1660 for the profits of the sequestered living. It was noted that in 1662 the church lacked a surplice for the rector, a book of homilies and Jewell's Apology. The last was a serious shortcoming. Dr John Jewell, Bishop of Salisbury from 1560 to 1571, had challenged 'Romanists' to prove their doctrines as well as opposing the Puritans, and his book *Apologia pro Ecclesia Anglicana*, written in Latin and published in 1562, stood at the heart of Anglicanism. No doubt these 'lacks' were made good and in 1730 a bequest in the will of John Townsend endowed the church with a fund to provide ten shillings for the annual preaching of a sermon on Good Friday.

The Civil War led to the loss of the church's chalice, made in 1553 and weighing 12 oz, because it was 'taken for the king'[148] and the present chalice, with patten cover, dates from 1661, immediately after the Restoration. The royal coat of arms hanging on the west wall of the nave dates from the reign of William and Mary (1685–1702) after the death of Mary in 1695.[149] The large tooled leather Bible on the brass eagle lectern was probably donated by Walter Pleydell-Bouverie and it was certainly originally presented to a relation of his – perhaps an uncle. The inscription, in gold letters on the inside, reads: 'Presented to General and Mrs Bouverie on the 50th Anniversary of their marriage by the inhabitants of Far Cotton in recognition of the kindness which prompted them to build a School Chapel for their use. April third 1866.' The two churchwardens' staves were the gift of John Wilfred Nosworthy and the embroidered 'kneelers' were the work of a group of ladies inspired in the 1970s by Beryl Hanna, the sister-in-law of the then rector, the Revd Pat Hanna.

The back benches of the choir stalls are old and may well date from the old church, but the stall stands for the choir would have been

148 *Victoria County History of Wiltshire*, p. 60.

149 Identification by Patrick Manley of Market Lavington in about 1997, when he cleaned it.

introduced after the nineteenth-century rebuilding. A second row of choir stalls, positioned in front of those still remaining, was removed as recently as the 1960s or 1970s. They testify to the existence, at one stage, of a choir of boys and men, although no one living now can remember it. Nevertheless it clearly flourished at one stage – perhaps between the 1880s and 1920s – as the churchwardens were billed on 13 August 1915 by Chas. H. Wood of Devizes for ten Cathedral psalters, three Hymns Ancient and Modern with tunes, and six hymn books for treble only. The hangings behind the altar were donated by Mrs Eileen Ross in memory of her husband Jim, a veterinary officer, who died in 2000.

BELLS

The two bells suspended from the original massive timbers in the tower are still rung each Sunday. They are believed to date from the early fourteenth century and to have been cast at a foundry in Salisbury. Certainly they were referred to in 1553 as 'continuing in existence' and Walters, the expert on Wiltshire bells, wrote of them:

> The smaller bell is early 14th century, with flat moulding round the shoulder, characteristic of that period. The other appears to be of about the same date, the only known parallel being one at Holdenhurst Hants. The larger bell, which has a shoulder like the smaller one, bears the inscription: + IESUS: NAZARENUS: REX: IVDEORUM: MISERERE: NOBIS [JESUS NAZARENUS REX JUDEORUM MISERERE NOBIS – Jesus of Nazareth, King of the Jews, have mercy upon us.]

The initial cross is apparently confined to a small group of early bells in this region.[150]

CLOCK

The present clock in the tower dates from 1887 and a brass plate on a beam adjoining the clock mechanism reads: 'This clock was erected in the Jubilee Year of Her Majesty Queen Victoria 1887 by the Parishioners of Little Cheverell and was made and fitted up by G.W. Blackie 392 Strand London.'

150 Walters, *Wiltshire Bells*, pp. 53, 251–3, 255.

The clock has a round face which was damaged shortly after installation by a village boy trying his new gun out by firing shots and causing three dents – later hammered out. The new clock replaced an earlier one installed at some unknown date, though it was already of some age in 1760, when there is a record of it being repaired. Unlike its successor, the earlier clock had – as shown both by the Buckler painting and a photograph taken perhaps in the 1870s – a diamond-shaped face, traces of which are still clearly visible on the stonework of the tower.

Maintenance of the clock was carried out by members of the Sainsbury family, followed by members of the Taylor family, the last to perform this service being Ken Taylor. From the middle 1980s it became the care of Wing Commander Victor King. The clock mechanism of brass and iron has been kept in pristine condition throughout and the face was repainted in 2005 by Captain K. Morison, RN.

THE ORGAN

The organ is a fine example of a small chamber organ, which, with five stops and no pedals, has beautiful tone and is reckoned to date from the mid-nineteenth century. It may previously have been in a house – not improbably Lavington Manor in the time of the Awdrys before they moved to Little Cheverell. The precise date of its installation in the chancel is uncertain but it was restored in 1982 at the instigation and expense of Colonel Rupert and Mrs Wheatley (formerly Margaret Newsom). This lady was a daughter of Alethea Newsom, *née* Awdry, and her husband the Revd George Newsom, Master of Selwyn College, Cambridge. A brass plaque on the organ itself reads:

In memory of Robert and Olive Awdry
Alethea Newsom and Helen Awdry
Who lived and worked in Wiltshire
For many years
This organ was restored in 1982

In 2006 the organ was completely rebuilt and the old casing finely renovated at a cost of more than £3,000 by the organ builder Stephen Cook – with the help of David Coram, who had played it as a boy – and repositioned in the south west of the nave. Vincent Gaiger on behalf of Gaiger Bros. also generously ensured that the incidental work necessary was rapidly completed.

In the days before the installation of the organ in the nineteenth century the music would no doubt have been provided, as was the practice in that epoch, by local musicians playing the violin and wind instruments. Neither personal memories nor records reveal much about organists before the 1930s and 1940s. Leathley Nightingale, who was musical director at Dauntsey's during the 1930s and 1940s, played during that period and one of his daughters sometimes pumped the bellows – a necessary function before an electrical pump was installed. In the 1950s two daughters of Bert Ridout were involved. Jean played the organ while her sister Pam (later the wife of Gordon Baker) did the pumping and for a spell then became organist herself. At this time she would sometimes cycle from work in the Devizes Telephone Exchange to play for the service and then cycle back to continue her work as a telephonist. Happily for the congregation she resumed her role as organist in the later 1990s and remains the organist today.[151]

In the intervening period Ivy Ladd, who with her husband Leonard lived at Meadow View,[152] was organist for many years. Sara Hawley assisted her from time to time for a year or two in the early 1980s and David Coram, a talented pupil from Dauntsey's School, now assistant organist at Romsey Abbey, was organist from 1995 to 1998.

CHURCHWARDENS

The care of church property, including the church itself and the churchyard, is the responsibility of two churchwardens elected annually. Some details are known about holders of this office but they are far from complete (Appendix E).

Churchwardens have to declare on appointment each year that they will 'faithfully and diligently discharge the duties' of their office and Phillimore's *Ecclesiastical Law*, the standard nineteenth-century work, defined these duties as 'to inspect the morals and behaviour of parishioners as well as to take care of the goods and repairs of the Church'. The former duty has happily been attenuated but maintenance of the church remains a prime duty. An idea, however, of what was expected

151 Pam Baker also brought her mother with her to services as long as she lived.
152 Where Michael and Linda Kavanagh now live. This house is not to be confused with Meadow View Cottage, the home of Martin and Sarah Walker.

of churchwardens of Little Cheverell in the first half of the nineteenth century can be gained from the questions put to them in the Archdeacon of Sarum's Visitation of 1833.

At that time, and for several decades subsequently, the parish clerk, who combined ecclesiastical and lay functions, was an important local personality who came after the clergy in ranking. One of the questions posed, therefore, was whether the parish clerk was of 'honest and sober conversation', sufficient for his reading, writing and – it is interesting to note – singing. Other questions were whether the churchwardens took such measures as the law prescribes to prevent tippling in public houses on the Lord's Day (fortunately no longer required of a churchwarden); whether there was a large Bible and Book of Common Prayer for the minister; on the arrangements for communion table rails; and whether the churchyard was kept free from all profane uses, particularly use as a playground or feeding cattle. A footnote on the questionnaire stated: 'Sheep are the only animals that ought to be permitted to feed in churchyards.'

All the answers were positive except one. The reply to the question about cattle in the churchyard was surprising for a village where sheep were an important part of the economy: 'Cows are occasionally had in it as it is impossible except at certain seasons to get fed by sheep.' The sheep were perhaps, at most times, up on the Plain.

PARISH AND BENEFICE

The small size of the parish has meant that it has at various times, and especially latterly, been held by a rector covering other parishes as well. As early as 1657 the Trustees for the Maintenance of Ministers recommended that the parishes of West Lavington and Little Cheverell should be united under one incumbent, although this did not come to pass until 1915, when Little Cheverell ceased to have a resident rector. So it continued until 1936 when these two parishes were held in plurality with Great Cheverell up to 1958. At this stage Little Cheverell was disunited from West Lavington but united with Great Cheverell until in 1965 Great Cheverell was separated again and the old dispensation of Little Cheverell being held with West Lavington was restored.

In 1981 West Lavington and the two Cheverells were grouped together once again and formed into the 'Benefice of West Lavington and the Cheverells'. The number of full-time clergy continued to decrease rapidly throughout the later part of the twentieth century and, after the Revd Terry Brighton left in 2002, the benefice was extended to include Market Lavington and Easterton with the Revd Harold Stephens as incumbent rector.

PATRONAGE

As emphasised earlier there was always, until comparatively recently, a close nexus between the manor and the church, particularly as the patronage of the living – the right to nominate the rector – lay with the lord of the manor. This remained the situation until, in 1915, Charles Awdry transferred it to the Bishop of Salisbury.

RECTORS, CURATES AND OTHERS

The names of the long line of rectors, who presided over all aspects of the church's affairs, are on record from as far back as 1297 – from Williamus de Lavington to the present incumbent, Harold Stephens. Similarly the names of those, separately appointed, to the Chantry of St Mary from the thirteenth to the fifteenth century are also known (Appendix F).

THE LIVES AND CHARACTERS OF RECTORS

Only two of Little Cheverell's clergy acquired very wide renown – Sir James Stonhouse in the late eighteenth century and a curate in the mid-twentieth century, the Revd Wilbert Awdry, author of *Thomas the Tank Engine*. A certain amount only is known about the lives of other rectors, although a number of them were men of some distinction. William of Lavington was not only rector of Little Cheverell but also responsible for a parish in Berkshire. Henry de la Forde, who was presented to the church in 1298, was apparently also briefly chaplain of the chantry for the Cheverell family. William Sumner, rector in 1458, was a theologian of repute and he was granted a dispensation to hold other parishes in plurality. In the Reformation period of the sixteenth century Little Cheverell was not immune from the conflict between Catholics and Protestants and the rector, Philip Stanlake, was a victim of this. Deposed in the reign of the Catholic Queen 'Bloody Mary' in favour of a Marian nominee, he was reinstated after the accession of the Protestant Queen Elizabeth I.

Hugh Gough, who was rector for a long period from 1584 to 1625 when the Hungerford family were lords of the manor, was fortunate also to be rector of All Cannings, another good living.[153] He was succeeded in 1625 by Roger Flower, who, already rector of Castle Combe, was presented by John Flower of Melksham. By exactly what power this was achieved is not clear, except that members of the Flower family seem to have had considerable influence in the local area at the time. This act of apparent nepotism, however, did not avail the incumbent, for the preparation of sermons does not seem to have been Roger Flower's strong point and he was dismissed for 'reading other men's works in the pulpit'. Nonetheless his son, who was also ordained, perhaps redeemed the family name by running a school at Chippenham. Another Flower – Steven fflower[154] – apparently lived in the village and was a churchwarden and benefactor of the parish. With his fellow churchwarden, John Still, he made a gift on 21 December 1654 of a 'Register Booke for the parish containing three and twentie leaves of parchment, besides the paper which cost three shillings'.

John Shergold, whose name was also spelt Shergoll or Shergull and who held the living between 1735 and 1759, was a local Wiltshire man. The son of John Shergold, a gentleman of Bishops Cannings, he went up to Trinity College, Oxford in 1713 aged sixteen, taking his BA in 1716 and MA in 1718. His first appointment was as vicar of Preston in Dorset from 1720 to 1722, after which he was appointed vicar of St John's, Devizes. He stayed in Devizes until 1738, during which time he sadly lost his first wife and baby son – there is a memorial to them in the south chancel of St John's. He married his second wife, Mary Still, in Devizes on 16 December 1731 at the age of thirty-four before moving on in 1735 to Little Cheverell, but there he was struck by further misfortune. Mary (Still) and two infant girls, also called Mary, died and were buried in a vault in the church. At least his daughter Ann, born in 1733 to his first wife, survived and she was married at the age of eighteen in Little Cheverell church on 29 December 1751 to James Sutton of Devizes. John Shergold was then appointed rector of Stanton St Quinton in 1759 and there he died on 24 December 1777.

He was succeeded as rector by John Newton, who held the living – as well as being vicar of Coleshill in Berkshire – between 1759 and 1764.

153 This term meant an ecclesiastical benefice or endowment.
154 Flower is spelt in this way in the official church record.

He is, however, not to be confused with his famous near-contemporary, who, having been captain of a slaving ship, repented, was ordained and wrote such well-known hymns as 'Glorious things of Thee are spoken' and 'How sweet the name of Jesus sounds'.

The next rector, Sir James Stonhouse (also sometimes spelt Stonehouse), who held the living from 1764 to 1796, was of considerable renown and it is intriguing to speculate on why the patron, Lord Radnor, appointed him. Born in 1716 and dying in 1795 he was the 11th baronet and it was he who substantially rebuilt the Rectory in 1782, living there at least part of the time for his remaining fourteen years. Stonhouse was also rector of Great Cheverell, where his curate, Mr Roots, lived in the Rectory. Sir James lived in Little Cheverell for only part of the year however, pleading to the Bishop that in winter 'being advanced in life and with this situation at the foot of the downs being very bleak, I am obliged to remove, during that time, and then reside at Bristol Wells'.

Sir James was the most famous of all the rectors and, well known both as physician and 'divine', found a place in the *Dictionary of National Biography*. Educated at St John's College, Oxford and French universities, he studied at St Thomas's Hospital in London and, between 1734 and 1763, practised medicine at Northampton, where he also founded the County Infirmary. At this time he fell under the influence of Philip Doddridge, a Nonconformist divine and academic. Doddridge was a presbyter of Northampton, a supporter of 'the dissenting interest', a Doctor of Divinity of Aberdeen University and also the author of books on the religion of the soul, pneumatology, ethics and divinity. It was he who inspired James Stonhouse to take holy orders in 1749, though Stonhouse continued to practise medicine and in 1758 attended James Hervey, the devotional writer – a contemporary of John Wesley at Lincoln College, Oxford – during his last illness.

When Sir James came to the West, he established himself as a well-known preacher in Bristol and Bath and in 1788 he published *Every Man's Assistant and the Sick Man's Friend*. Like Dr Johnson, David Garrick, William Wilberforce and John Newton, the former ship-captain, he was a friend of Hannah More,[155] who much admired him and gave him the sobriquet of 'The Shepherd of Salisbury Plain'. A fluent and prolific authoress and playwright, she also mastered Italian,

155 1745–1833.

Spanish and Latin. One of the early founders of Sunday schools, she was also a benefactor who left £30,000 to charitable institutions and religious societies.

The titles of the works of those intimately involved, and passionately engaged, in the religious revival of the late eighteenth and early nineteenth centuries would scarcely have produced bestsellers in the twenty-first century and their effect on the people of Little and Great Cheverell is apparently unrecorded. Few would have read them but indirectly such works may have been influential, as Sir James's fame as a preacher may have drawn quite large congregations in an era when village churchgoers expected a long sermon. No one doubts how effectively the preaching of John and Charles Wesley in the West Country inspired huge crowds. Whatever the numbers, however, James Stonhouse records that he always administered the sacraments at the four great festivals of Easter, Christmas, Whitsun and Trinity and preached the annual Good Friday sermon.

Other details of his pastoral life in Little Cheverell are brought out in his responses to the questions posed in the Bishop's Visitation in 1783. To questions about whether there were any reputed Papists or Presbyterians, Independents, Anabaptists or Quakers in the parish, Stonhouse was able to give a categorical 'no'. As for the inquiry whether parishioners sent their children and servants, who had not learned their catechism, to him to be instructed, he had to answer 'Not as many as I could wish ...but as many as generally in parishes of this size.'

Strangely Sir James was not the only one called 'the Shepherd of Salisbury Plain' for the tomb memorial for David Saunders of Littleton Panell reads:

Erected in the Year 1829
To the Memory of
DAVID SAUNDERS

Known through every Quarter of the Globe
Under the appellation of
THE PIOUS SHEPHERD OF SALISBURY PLAIN
Whose little History has now been read with
Admiration by Multitudes of Christians
In EUROPE, ASIA, AFRICA AND AMERICA
He was buried here by his Sons
Sepr. 9th 1796. Aged 70.

Sir James Stonhouse's successor, the Revd William Richards, who held the living for twenty-seven years from 1796 to 1823, was generally more in the mould of a normal country rector, but he became involved in the complicated exchanges of land made at the time of the Inclosures and the increase in the parsons' glebe. For three years after that the Revd Joseph P. Griffith had the living; his initials are inscribed on the north wall of the kitchen of Little Cheverell House when this was added in the 1820s.

The initials 'JRF', on the other hand, inscribed on the wall of that part of Cheverell Place which formed the old Rectory stables, are those of the Revd John Roles Fishlake. Rector from 1826, he held the living for forty-one years until 1867, a very popular man who was 'much loved by his flock'.[156] He is buried in the churchyard. His successor, the Revd William Powley Nichols of Worcester College, Oxford, was rector for even longer, no less than forty-six years. A bachelor of somewhat eccentric manners, he was renowned in the village for preaching with wide-open eyes fixed on the roof and never looking at his congregation at all. He was, however, a talented watercolourist who concentrated largely on local landscapes, as well as an avid collector of antiquities. It is interesting to note that his income in 1898 was £405 from 190 acres of Glebe[157] but he was the last resident rector. Like his predecessor, he too was buried in the churchyard. On his death, the next rector, the Revd Henry Margesson, put the Rectory on the market on the instructions of Salisbury Diocese and it was sold by auction at the Bear Hotel in Devizes on 9 December 1915.

After Henry Margesson, the Revd Canon Percival Sexty was rector for thirty-two years, 1926 to 1958, and he is remembered by older villagers with affection, especially because he used to visit them regularly. His successor, the Revd Canon Pat Hanna, a bachelor, also became a much-loved rector and it was only after a stroke in 1982 that he had to retire. His effectiveness was enhanced by the support given by his sister, Nancy, and brother Jim, whose wife Beryl organised and inspired a number of local initiatives. Happily his successor was the Revd Maurice Osborn, who was already well known as a former chaplain and history master at Dauntsey's School. He was also very popular and loved, not least for his incisive but brief sermons,

156 Evidently told to the ladies who compiled ' History of Little Cheverell'.
157 *Crockford's Directory*.

never lasting more than about eight minutes and always directly relevant to current events. Though their length might have disappointed a Victorian congregation, they were made more lively by being delivered without a note, except for assistance with an occasional quotation.

The Revd Hugh Hoskins, the next rector, was a man in a different mould. An industrial chemist before taking orders, he introduced a note of modern enthusiasm and, whilst adjusting well to a comparatively conservative congregation, he and his wife inspired young people into activity within the church. He was followed by the Revd Terry Brighton, who, proud of his Yorkshire origins and straight talking, made his mark locally before moving to a parish in Devon.

OTHER PRIESTS AND PEOPLE INVOLVED

The earlier rectors had curates who took some services. John Lewis, for instance, signed registers as curate in 1636 and 1637 and Timothy Stonhouse, a son or other relative of Sir James, was also curate in the latter eighteenth century and was buried at Little Cheverell in 1767.

The ordination of women as priests, first permitted in 1994,[158] introduced a profound change and in 2002 the Revd Pam Smith became the first female priest to administer to the parish as well as the other parishes in the benefice, living in the former vicarage of West Lavington on a 'house for duty' basis. Much loved and respected in her three years period of office, she was known not only for taking and preaching at many church services but also as a pastoral visitor. After she left to become a full-time stipendiary priest, two other women joined the benefice clergy in 2004 and 2005 as non-stipendiary priests – the Revd Anne Cocking and the Revd Pat Strowger.

Services in the 1980s and earlier were sometimes taken by a lay reader, John Titt. A quiet man, he is remembered, among other things, for always arriving from West Lavington where he lived on a bicycle and wearing bicycle clips, of a sort seldom seen any more, for his trousers. In the 1990s Margaret Wheatley and the author were both

158 The canon making this possible was promulgated in the General Synod of the Church of England in February 1994 and the first thirty-two women priests were ordained on 12 March 1994.

licensed by the Bishop of Salisbury to take Matins services, when some desire for these to be reinstated was expressed.

NATURE OF SERVICES

In medieval times the church was perhaps the scene of the miracle plays common at the time. Certainly, before the Reformation in the sixteenth century the Catholic mass in Latin would always have been celebrated, and it was probably last held in 1558 at the end of Queen Mary's reign. From then on, for four centuries, worship was exclusively from the Prayer Book of 1662, based on Archbishop Cranmer's earlier work, and the Authorised Version of the Bible, approved by King James I.

The importance attached to strict observance of this prescribed form of worship is demonstrated by the Archdeacon of Sarum's Visitation in 1833, when the churchwardens were asked 'whether the incumbent was of exemplary life and conversation and did he properly robed perform devoutly and audibly the service of the Church as prescribed by the Book of Common Prayer without adding diminishing or altering?' The churchwardens were – perhaps fortunately for all concerned – able to answer 'yes' and they also gave an affirmative answer to 'whether there was regular both morning and evening service, whether a sermon was preached at least once every Sunday and whether Holy Communion was ministered so often and at such stated seasons that every Parishioner may communicate at least thrice every year'. The Communion was largely confined to the great feasts and festivals of the church, as shown by James Stonhouse's reply to the question in the Bishop of Salisbury's 'Visitation' of 1783 quoted above.

The biggest changes in the form of worship came after the Second World War although, until about the 1960s, morning and evening services were still regularly held on Sundays and the communion service, or Eucharist, was not held nearly as frequently as now. From the 1960s onwards, however, the Eucharist became the principal feature of Sunday service in Little Cheverell in accordance with successive 'experimental' services introduced into the church until the Alternative Service Book, in traditional language, was adopted. Common Worship was introduced for the whole of the Church of England in 2000 and it, together with the Book of Common Prayer, contains the texts now authorised for all services.

In Little Cheverell innovation is blended with tradition, because the

Book of Common Prayer is used both for communion services at 8 a.m. once a month and also the periodic Matins services, while the traditional language form of 'Holy Communion Order One' from Common Worship is followed for the other two weekly services on Sundays at 11 a.m. Bible readings at services are frequently, but by no means exclusively, taken from the traditional Authorised Version. The church has followed a broad ecumenical approach since at least the early 1990s and all members of the village, of whatever denomination, are welcomed, especially to the Little Cheverell Harvest Festival service and the Crib service held on Christmas Eve.

THE CHURCH CONGREGATION

It is difficult to establish the size of congregations in the church in former times, but Sir James Stonhouse, in his reply to the Bishop's inquiries in 1783, listed the number of communicants over a three year period:

1781	Easter	35	Whitsun	33	Michaelmas	34	Christmas	28
1782		22		34		31		22
1783		32		24				

He noted, however, that attendance at the service at which the Good Friday sermon, endowed by John Townsend, was preached was not so impressive: 'very few attend as no notice is taken of that day by the working people of this neighbourhood, whose bread depends on their labour.' The relative poverty of the congregation is also revealed by the answer to the question 'By whom, and to what uses, is the money given at the offertory disposed?': 'None has ever been collected, as this parish is so circumstanced that none can afford to give: chiefly cottagers, and a few farmers, who are renters.'[159]

There is no doubt that church attendance in the eighteenth and early nineteenth centuries was considerably higher than it is now and villagers still living in the 1950s recalled that, in their lifetime, the two Sunday services were well attended. They also recalled that the popular Harvest Home suppers after the Harvest Festival service were particularly memorable, remembering with nostalgic humour and indulgence

159 A reference to the fact that the farmers were copyhold tenants and not freeholders.

one unnamed man who indulged himself so freely at one of these suppers that he lost his way in Shovel Wood on the way home. Although his cries for help were, for a while, merely mocked by an owl, nearby cottagers eventually heard, rescued him and set him back on course.[160]

In recent years the congregation has been small but attendance, usually about fifteen, has been at a relatively high level compared with the national average. Only a small number of the present congregation were either born in the village or have been very long-term residents. One is Greta Taylor, a long-term member of the Parochial Church Council, who has also been one of those who carry out sacristan duties. Another well-established member of the Council, Olive Cox, has been a very devoted cleaner of the church and a major provider of home-made marmalade for the annual church bazaar in November. Her daughter Stephanie, who was married in the church in 2004, has for several years been narrator at the Christmas Crib services. Apart from her involvement in the church, she obtained a catering degree, became the caterer for the Urchfont College and also started a local catering business which, with the help of her mother and other members of the family, has come to provide teas for the Wiltshire Archers Tennis Club – which incidentally was founded considerably earlier than Wimbledon!

THE RECTORY

The rector of Little Cheverell's house was always a significant one in the village and it stood for many centuries on or near the site of Little Cheverell House, which was the Rectory from at least the late eighteenth century until 1915. Some details have been preserved of earlier parsonage houses on the site and, in 1608, the rector's home was a 'Glebe-House', consisting of seven bays in a half quadrangle, together with a court adjoining the dwelling house, an orchard and a hop garden. There were also stables, cowhouse, carthouse, rick barton[161] adjoining a barn, and a barton to feed cattle in winter.[162]

There does not seem to have been much change for many decades, for the parsonage house was still on the same site in 1671, and by the

160 'Little Cheverell Village History'.
161 A barton was a farmyard.
162 Stephen Hobbs (ed.), *Wiltshire Glebe Terriers*, Wiltshire Record Society 2003, no. 149, p. 79.

1720s the property was described as consisting of a house, barn, stables, 'backside', orchard and gardens covering two acres. Traces of some of these earlier outbuildings are still visible and an interesting feature, possibly dating back to the sixteenth or seventeenth centuries, is a small patio area adjoining Little Cheverell House on the south side. Its formal shape, with large numbers of flat stone slates stuck into the ground on their sides to make hard paths between what were originally perhaps oblong, round and half-moon flower beds, suggests that it may once have been an Elizabethan herb garden.

The house in its present form began to take shape in 1782 when Sir James Stonhouse rebuilt it to suit his personal needs. He added a kitchen block to parts of the existing stone building which still remained at the south end, though this was replaced a few years later. The middle part of the new house was built in 1783 and Sir James described the operation in his report to the Bishop of Salisbury in 1783:[163]

> Parsonage house:- last year there were 4 rooms added to the parsonage, the plan of it before the alteration and after is in your lordship's registry together with the dimension of the room, material and every other circumstance. This spring I have rebuilt the middle part of the house, the inside of which will be finished in about a month. The dimensions of the bed chamber are 19ft. 7 ins. by 15 ft. 2 ins. floored with deal. Under that is a passage and laundry, paved with square paving brick, and servants' pantry, floored with elm. The house is built of brick with freestone quoins, freestone window frames etc. There is part of the building standing at the end of rough stone plastered over and drawn with lines so as to resemble brick, consisting of offices and servants' rooms. The house is covered with brick tiles.

Sir James, whose attention to detail was marked, also described the rest of the property as 'one large barn – with two threshing floors – '84 ft. by 23 ft. boarded floor, brick and stone foundation to the external building, the rest board and thatched, skilling to 24 ft. by 9 ft. Stable 44 ft. by 17 ft. built with brick and thatched, stall for 8 horses.' There was also a Court house[164] 49ft. by 11 ft. supported by oak posts and

163 *Ibid.*, 153, p. 85.

164 It is not clear whether or not this was used as a court house for the manorial court for business concerning the village.

thatched. There was no granary when Sir James came to the Rectory although, curiously, there was 'one on the premises but belonging to the tenant'.

Further additions to the house were made in the nineteenth century and, after it ceased to be a rectory in 1915, a billiards room which later became a drawing room was built on with a bedroom above by Admiral John Luce in the early 1920s. The eighteenth-century style and tradition of craftsmanship was nonetheless maintained and, despite its elongation, the house remains homogenous and harmonious. In the 1960s Joyce Lady Crossley had a number of higgledy-piggledy rooms, mainly nineteenth-century servants' quarters, removed from the back of the house which was thus restored to its earlier classical shape, matching the façade.

THE OLD RECTORY – LITTLE CHEVERELL HOUSE

Since the Rectory was sold in Devizes in 1915 the property has been in private hands. The owners of Little Cheverell House since then have been:

Mr John George Perret[165]
Rear Admiral John Luce and later Mrs Luce (1924–39/40)
Dr F. L. Newton Dunn (1939/40–63)
Joyce Lady Crossley (1963– 80)
Sir Donald and Lady Hawley (1980–2002)
Mr Jonathan Pye (2002–)

The Perrets, who had moved from Coulston, sold the property to Rear Admiral John Luce, a retired Royal Navy officer with deep family roots in Wiltshire – especially at Malmesbury, where the church contains a number of Luce family memorials. Admiral Luce, who commanded HMS *Glasgow* at the Battle of Coronel and the Falklands in 1914, was at Clifton College at the same time as Sir Henry Newbolt, who wrote the famous poem 'Drake's Drum', and in a letter to the poet written from HMS *Ramillies* on 16 February 1919 the Admiral drew his attention to the belief of some senior naval officers that they had heard the legendary drum at the end of the war:

165 Information given in Catherine Nosworthy's memorandum.

Dear Sir Henry Newbolt,

I do not know whether the following story, which I believe has appeared in a provincial paper, has come to your notice – if not it may possibly interest you. On the occasion when the Grand Fleet put to sea to meet and bring in the surrendered German High Sea Fleet, the Captain of one of our newest battleships, which took part, had as a guest on board for the occasion the Captain of a sister ship which was refitting in dock at the time and was thus unable to be present at the surrender.

During the day these officers noticed a peculiar sound of a drumming nature which both remarked on. It was described as a drum beat of a ceremonial or stately sound. The Captain of the ship made enquiries as to what it could be, thinking it might be some sound in the ship, though it was unfamiliar to him, but nothing could be found to which it could be attributed. Was this Drake's Drum?

The two officers who heard it had each commanded ships in the Battle of Jutland, and have since left the Grand Fleet.

You will not know my name, but I can remember you in the 6th Form at Clifton, when I was a small boy in the Junior School.

Yours sincerely,

John Luce

This phenomenon was also mentioned by Pamela Glenconner in a letter to Sir Henry Newbolt dated 20 June 1919. Captain Maclaughlan, she said, had confirmed that a drum was heard on his ship, HMS *Royal Oak*, and that the matter was all the more mysterious because every sailor was at his action station at the time.[166]

Admiral John Luce played a prominent part in Wiltshire after his retirement from the Royal Navy. High Sheriff in 1930 and a governor of Dauntsey's School, he is still remembered in the village for his stentorian 'quarterdeck' voice, put to good use to deter mischievous boys from appropriating apples in his orchard.[167] His daughter-in-law,

166 *The Later Life and Letters of Sir Henry Newbolt*, edited by his wife Margaret, pp. 263, 408 and 409. The author was told about Drake's Drum in the early 1930s by the headmaster of Elstree, his prep school, Lieutenant Commander Ian Sanderson, an officer who had served at the Battle of Jutland in 1916 and appeared to believe in the tradition that the drum was heard as a rallying call when England was being challenged at sea.

167 A recollection of John Oram given to the author.

Margaret,[168] had a distinct recollection of Little Cheverell House in the admiral's day. On a warm afternoon when she and her future husband William[169] were standing outside, she suggested that it was perhaps time for India to be given its independence. She had not noticed that the Admiral was half asleep in a chair nearby, under his panama hat, and her remark caused a sudden explosion: 'I suppose you want to give away the whole bloody British Empire!'

Two of the admiral's four sons were particularly well known. Admiral Sir David Luce, who later lived at Bratton, became First Sea Lord but, disagreeing with the then government's policy over aircraft carriers which he believed were essential for Britain's defence, he resigned. Sir William Luce had a distinguished overseas career, first in the Anglo-Egyptian Government of the Sudan and later as Governor of Aden and then H. M. Political Resident in the Persian Gulf. After final retirement he became Special Adviser to the Secretary of State, Sir Alec Douglas-Home, on Middle Eastern Affairs in the later 1960s and early 1970s. His son, Richard, Lord Luce, became Lord Chamberlain after a varied political, overseas and academic life.

After the death of Admiral John Luce in 1932, Mrs Luce continued to live at Little Cheverell House and not only took part in local affairs but was also reputed as a very good and keen gardener, as well as a violinist in the Dauntsey's School Orchestra. The next owner, Dr F. L. Newton Dunn, was a prominent Salisbury doctor and Lady Crossley, who bought the house from him, was the widow of Sir Herbert Crossley, Bt., the inventor and founder of Crossley cars, a famous British make before the Second World War. A notable plantswoman, she collected specimens from all over the world and not only opened the garden of Little Cheverell House to the public once a year but was also the organiser of the National Gardens Scheme in Wiltshire.

It was pure but happy chance which caused the author and his wife Ruth to buy the house in 1980, for his career had overlapped with that of Sir William Luce both in the Sudan and the Diplomatic Service. After retirement from the Diplomatic Service in 1981, the author became, *inter alia*, President of the Council of Reading University and Chairman of the Sir William Luce Memorial Fund at Durham University. Lady

168 Lady Luce, wife of Sir William Luce, was the daughter of Admiral Sir Trevelyan Napier, KCB. She told the author the story.
169 Later Sir William Luce.

(Ruth) Hawley was very active and prominent in public affairs in Wiltshire. Already very heavily engaged with St John Ambulance and the Order of St John of Jerusalem, as County Commander, County President and a regional representative on the Council of the Priory of England, she became High Sheriff in 1998/9 and subsequently a Deputy Lieutenant. Fully involved in church life, she also became a lay canon of Salisbury Cathedral in 2000.

In 2001 the property of Little Cheverell House was divided into two and the Hawleys sold the main house, with about two acres, but retained the old rector's coach house, built in 1836, as well as the barn, cow shed and some other outbuildings, together with the rest of the land including the north-west paddock. A new house, designed by the architect Gerald Steer of Salisbury, was built by Gaiger Brothers of Devizes in classical early eighteenth-century style and grafted on to the coach house. The Hawleys moved into it on 4 September 2001 and called it Cheverell Place. In 2003 the barn was also converted into living space with two bedrooms, a living room, dining room and kitchen as an adjunct of Cheverell Place. The landscaped garden was created out of the former paddock and a number of trees planted, including a cedar of Lebanon.

THE LATTER DAYS OF OLD-STYLE FARMING: THE NOSWORTHY FARM

From 1914 onwards the greater part of the land and property in and around the village was owned by John Nosworthy, who farmed Manor Farm until he died in 1927. All this was then inherited by his son John Wilfred Nosworthy and it is therefore no surprise that the name of Nosworthy crops up in most people's recollections of earlier twentieth-century days.

John Nosworthy, who had come to the area from Manaton in Devon, at first farmed a considerable area as a tenant of the lord of the manor, Charles Awdry, but disliking this status, he was keen to buy the land. In 1914 he had his opportunity when the whole Lavington estate was put up for sale at auction, and he seized it by acquiring ownership of the greater part of Little Cheverell as well as considerable land elsewhere. His acquisitions in Little Cheverell were completed by his purchase of Glebe Farm from his friends the Bazells, who nevertheless stayed on as his tenants. Clearly a determined man, he was renowned for his managerial gifts and keeping careful accounts of all his operations, to which might be added his pride in owning good buildings and having everything in ship-shape order.[170]

He may perhaps have been on slightly uneasy terms with the vendor's family and apparently shouted one day at Robert Awdry, who was walking with dogs over his recently acquired land. On the other hand Catherine Nosworthy, his granddaughter, was told as a girl that the Awdrys and her grandfather and grandmother had been picnicking together when Olive Awdry, the Colonel's wife, had been 'very taken' with the present site of Hawkswell House for their new home – as it in time became.

John Nosworthy's possessiveness over land was one reason why he bought a substantial farm for his son at Stanton St Bernard near Pewsey, although John Wilfred never moved there. He preferred instead to live at Highfield House, Great Cheverell and, when his father died, he was only too happy to move again into Manor Farm, where he had lived as a child.

The characters of John and of John Wilfred Nosworthy were very different and the latter, unlike his father, 'would not say boo to a goose',[171] and left a reputation as a kindly man, who played an important part in village life. His daughter Catherine, recalling that the working people seemed to her very poor and thin, believed that her father kept many men on the payroll who did not have very much to do, in order to alleviate their poverty.

Before the Second World War there were still many thousand working horses on farms in Wiltshire and, in the late 1930s, there were about twelve shire horses on the Nosworthy farm. All of these were required when the heavy threshing machinery had to be hauled up 'White Road' for harvesting on the Plain.[172] The horses were also used to pull wagons in the harvest fields, and local lads always looked forward to earning a little pocket money from 'wagging on' by leading them from one set of stooks to another to facilitate loading.

Despite the Secomd World War, life for the majority of people in Little Cheverell carried on for a number of years after it, in many ways

170 The accounts etc were deposited in the County Archives.

171 Memorandum given to the author by Catherine Nosworthy, daughter of John Wilfred Nosworthy, in 2000.

172 Recollections of Ken Taylor and of Harold Beaven. The white road was apparently the road now in the possession of the MOD leading up to the Plain.

as it had before, revolving round the farms. Several people still living in the village in 2006 can recall the days when the huge farm horses were still working and later grazing in the fields near the church in their final retirement.[173] Olive Cox regarded John Wilfred Nosworthy's keeping on old pensioned horses in this way, when tractors were becoming more common, as typical of his kindness.

Apart from the heavy shire horses, John Wilfred Nosworthy had another lighter one called 'Charlie'. This was used by Lewis Draper every Thursday to drive to Devizes in a light four-wheeled wagon, laden with goods for the market and to bring back livestock acquired. Although Charlie was a light enough horse to trot quite rapidly, the whole outing in fact took most of the day. His stable was at the rear of the farmhouse whereas the shire horses were stabled near the front gates.[174] They were all kept shod by Percy Kellaway, the blacksmith in West Lavington.

John Wilfred Nosworthy's daughter, Catherine, who grew up at Manor Farm House, still recalls something of her life there in those stricter days, when social divisions were still quite marked. She and her sister Judith were not allowed to speak to any of the men or to go on to the farm during working hours. Another vivid memory is of Mrs Wilkins, who lived in one of the nearby cottages now demolished and came to the farmhouse to do the washing – using a 'blue bag and filling the place with steam when she heated the copper'.[175]

Catherine Nosworthy's great-grandparents had lived at Littleton House and, after the death of her grandfather John Nosworthy in 1927, his widow Elizabeth (Bessie), who was one of the family of Dr D. W. Butler of Rowde, went to live at Littleton Lodge. This grandmother used to cycle over to Manor Farm on Sunday afternoons to see the family and also to give Catherine and her sister Judith Scripture lessons.

The countryside was then a great deal quieter than now,[176] for there were few tractors, roads were free of cars except for very occasional light traffic, and bicycles were in general use. Another difference between then and now is the physical change in the village's appearance, due the loss of all the elm trees caused by Dutch elm disease in the

173 For example Olive Cox's recollections narrated to the author.
174 Recollections of Bruce Nightingale and Ken Taylor and Olive Cox.
175 'Coppers' to heat the water were indispensable for laundering until the age of the washing machine.
176 Memoirs of Bruce Nightingale.

1970s. These included a double row of elms on the driveway from the Westbury road to the Manor Farm House and a number in the grounds of Little Cheverell House.[177]

Olive Cox (*née* Page) recalls[178] that, when she first came to the village as the bride of Bill Cox in 1947, twenty or thirty men still worked regularly on the Nosworthy farm, including George Cox, her father-in-law, who was one of the shepherds. His full name was William George Cox and he came to the village at the age of twenty from Enford to take his job as shepherd, starting his new employment, as was customary for centuries in England, at Michaelmas. Before moving to one of the estate houses on the Westbury road, he lived with his wife at Laundry Cottage, where Mrs Nurse subsequently lived,[179] and in his work he shared, with Percy Baker and 'Snowy' Chapman, the task of shearing sheep, looking after their tails and keeping their feet free from rot. George Cox kept his rams on Cheverell Cliff, before it was planted with trees, and his sheep grazed on the uplands over as far as New Zealand Farm as well as on land at Tilshead, owned by J. W. Nosworthy.[180] The leading ewe of a flock always had a bell, made in Great Cheverell by the Lancaster family, and, even when the red flag flew to indicate that firing was taking place on the ranges, the sheep would still graze on unconcernedly.

George Cox was 'a real old Wiltshireman', who throughout his life spoke the broad Wiltshire dialect, often leaving Olive Cox, accustomed as she then was to London accents and never acquiring an old Wiltshire accent herself, at a loss as to what he meant. He would, for instance, refer to his ewes as 'Yose' and, if he were going to Devizes, he would say he was 'going "Vizes"'. Sometimes too he would laughingly clap his hands and say to her: 'Thee's a capper. Thee'st make I laugh,' which might be translated as: 'You're the tops. You make me laugh.' Other interesting forms of earlier local usage were recorded by the rector in the 1860s, although it is not clear how long they persisted. 'Being in a caddle' meant 'wearing untidy costume' and 'a main few' was used for 'a considerable number'. But the once general voices of villagers such

177 The author and his wife took over a large store of elm wood logs on their purchase of Little Cheverell House in 1980.
178 An oral account to the author on Sunday 14 May 2000 in the churchyard.
179 Now owned by Peter and Rachel Dee-Shapland.
180 Oral testimony of Olive Cox.

as George Cox and Ted Wilkins, one of the last 'local characters' who died in 1998, have faded away and the rich, and to some unintelligible, old Wiltshire dialect is seldom if ever heard any more.

As for cattle in the Nosworthys' time, Ted, who was one of several Wilkinses working on the farm, was the last traditional cowman and he continued to milk the cows himself till the end. Although he eventually took charge of all the cows, he started work under his uncle 'Old Ernie' Wilkins, head cowman after the Second World War, who lived close to his cows in a cottage demolished in the 1970s, then standing between Glebe Farm House and the 'Ministry of Defence' houses. 'Old Ernie's' son, 'Young Ernie', served in the Army in the Second World War but returned to work on the farm and Ted Wilkins was given responsibility for the small calves which were kept in the yard where The Chimes and West House now stand opposite the church. The larger calves were kept in a barn, also since demolished, standing close to Pillar Box Cottage, which now belongs to Helena Warnock.[181] The large numbers of cattle, however, moving between the farm and their pastures left the road so soiled that it was almost unusable by pedestrians.

The cattle obviously needed water and this was the job of Ed Hargreaves, the Nosworthys' carter, who filled a large barrel on wheels, drawn by a horse, from the carriage ford on the Hawkswell stream opposite Bridge House.[182] He lived at Hargreaves Cottage, a thatched cottage formerly standing behind the black barn near Bridge House, but this too has been demolished.

Manor Farm was bought by the War Department by compulsory purchase – probably in 1934 with other land – but John Wilfred Nosworthy continued to farm it as a tenant, his main crops being the traditional ones of wheat, barley, potatoes and turnips.[183] When John Wilfred Nosworthy died in 1972, Alan Harley, a Scot, became tenant of the farm and he gave up the dairy herd to concentrate on beef cattle, farming much of the upland on lease from the Ministry of Defence, as the Nosworthys had continued to do after the War Department acquired it earlier. Alan Harley was subsequently able to buy much of the land.

181 Recollections of Greta Taylor and Helena Warnock.
182 Information given to the author by Greta Taylor on 19 July 2004.
183 *Kelly's Directory* for 1935.

The difference, as people still alive have witnessed, between the farming methods of their earlier days and those of 2006 is immense. The greatest change of all locally came in John Wilfred Nosworthy's time when working horses were replaced by tractors on the farm. Already by the mid 1940s he was using them more generally, though they were unsophisticated in comparison with their modern successors. It is now difficult to imagine that they ran on 'TVO' (tractor vaporising oil), and that the drivers had to start them up with petrol, switching them over to TVO by turning a tap as soon as the engines were sufficiently warm. The older ways have, however, now become a distant memory, with one man working great areas requiring several farm hands in the past, and huge, noisy agricultural machines dominating the scene.

FRANK BEAVEN'S FARM

Between the 1920s and 1950s another smaller farm had a particular place in village life. The name of Beaven in some form has been known in the village since at least the seventeenth century and the red house to the north of Sheep Drove opposite the gate of Cheverell Place (originally the back gate to Little Cheverell House) was built for Frank Beaven early in the 1930s by the builders Hillier Brown. Now called Kit Farm, it was originally called South View Farm and consisted of the farm house and a smallholding of some forty acres of land which had been part of the rector's Glebe until it was sold in 1915.

Frank Beaven married Beatrice Yeoman of Trowbridge and they brought up their family, of three sons and one daughter, on South View Farm. William became a policeman and rose to become a police sergeant; Walter farmed Warren Farm in Savernake Forest, and the daughter Evelyn became a nurse, met and married a sergeant in the US forces during the Second World War and went with him to live in the US. The other son, Harold,[184] was born at the farm but left it to become

184 The manner by which this account was obtained was strange. The author was at a function at Reading University, at which the Personal Assistant to the Registrar, Mary Maclean, said that her mother, who had come from Little Cheverell, would like to meet him. When they were introduced she disclosed that she had known Furze Hill Farm from her childhood. The author asked her if she would contribute her recollections but she passed the task to Harold Beaven, her brother-in-law.

an engine driver and spend forty-two years on the railways, first with the GWR and then British Rail. The nature of the job changed during this time and at first he drove steam engines, wearing overalls for the dirty work which that entailed. When diesels replaced steam engines, however, the drivers were issued with two new uniform suits a year of which he still retains a sample.[185]

Frank Beaven invariably got up, without benefit of alarm clock, on the dot of 5 a.m. He owned a herd of about twenty, including four or so milking cows, but the farm was devoted mainly to market gardening – vegetables, turnips, swedes and potatoes. Frank Beaven himself and other members of the family distributed milk in the village and, going round with two large buckets on the handlebars of a bicycle, filled the jugs of customers left out on their doorsteps. Sometimes the buckets were cooled by putting them in the pellucidly clear spring opposite Springside Cottage. Market produce was taken by the Beavens' horse-drawn cart to Lavington station, where it was shipped by train via Westbury to a wholesaler named Hill in Cardiff.

Frank Beaven was popular with workers from the village who came at harvest time, which became an essentially social occasion on his farm. His popularity was enhanced by the ever-present barrel of cider, from which they were free to take swigs without payment, and even local policemen were not averse to taking advantage of his liberality. The Beavens also derived a little humour from the visible and audible clashes of personalities in the grounds of Little Cheverell House between Mrs Newton Dunn and her daughter Margaret on the one hand and their donkey, 'Agnes', on the other. Prone to escape from time to time, the creature merely kicked up her heels in response to attempts to recapture her – a reaction which drove Mrs Newton Dunn to somewhat noisy fury.[186]

Harold Beaven's wife, Evelyn, was the granddaughter of W. C. (Charles) Turner who owned Furze Hill Farm and the adjacent brick-works. She recalls that this farm was run by her Uncle Frank Turner and Aunt Min, the father and mother of Robert Turner. She described it as being quite simple, with a kitchen and an Aga, a walk-in larder, a living room and a sitting room, but modern bathroom facilities were

185 Memoirs of Harold Beaven, who was born at South View Farm in 1953 and grew up there from 1933 to 1953. He retains a sample of his uniform as a memento.
186 Recollections of Harold Beaven.

lacking. Baths were taken in a tin bath in front of the fire and the earth closet was outside.

Peter Edwards, now living at Kit Farm, became in the mid-1990s a tenant of Arthur Pocock, who had bought the farm from the Beaven family for £5,000. A connection of Frank Beaven's, he now farms several hundred acres in Wiltshire in partnership with Lyn Rooke who, with her husband Gill, lives at Hawkswell Stables.

THE TURNERS

The Turner family farmed not only Furze Hill Farm (sometimes known as Turner's Farm), close to the former brickworks, but also Hillside Farm close by. Robert Turner, who still lives in the village and has in the past been a member both of the parish council and the parochial church council, was the last to farm Hillside.

THE EDWARDSES

Ken Edwards[187] took over Marlen in Low Road from his father Leonard and mother Mary who bought it in 1931 as a small holding for £99, which was a man's annual wage in those days. It had earlier belonged to Ken's uncle Frank Beaven, who moved to his new house, South View Farm, at about the same time. The name of the house was a contraction of the Christian names of Mary and Leonard Edwards, who had earlier lived in the Glebe Farm house of Great Cheverell, of which only a few stones now remain in a wood, situated east of Pear Tree Hill.

The family had an eight acre holding, the greater part of which was rented from Frank Beaven near South View Farm and they worked very hard to grow sugar beet, which was sold to Kidderminster, and vegetables such as parsnips, carrots and turnips, sold to 'middlemen' who supplied the retail greengrocers. Ken and Mary lived at Marlen until 1996, when they moved to Market Lavington; but Ken recalls an interesting detail about local farming methods. There was once a hatch a little upstream from their house, the purpose of which was to control the flow of the stream to flood a water meadow, when appropriate.

187 Ken Edwards gave an account of his life on a TV programme called *Little Cheverell*, and broadcast on local television.

OTHER RECOLLECTIONS OF FORMER TIMES

Other recently collected personal recollections of people still living in the village or living in the village at the time, together with stories told to them by their elders and photographs of their forebears, offer further glimpses of village life in earlier days, particularly from the 1920s to the 1960s.

BOLTERS AND BOULTERS

Although some people still alive in 2006 remember members of the Bolter family living in the village, no one of this name remains. This is the more remarkable in view of their establishment in the village since the sixteenth century, their former prominence and their numbers. By 1800, as mentioned above, of the 183 people living in 43 houses, 22 had the name of Bolter (or Boulter). By 1851 that figure had risen to 56 or 22% of the village and, when the Lavington Manor Estate was sold in July 1914, no fewer than five properties in Little Cheverell were let to people with this name. When the school closed in 1921, there were two Bolter boys in the school.[188] Joseph Bolter was among those from the village killed in the First World War and George Bolter was the only Little Cheverell man killed on active service in the Second World War – in Italy near Monte Cassino.[189]

The name of Bolter possibly originates from the skill of making bolts or arrows for crossbows, *le boltere*, and in the seventeenth and eighteenth centuries there was considerable variation in the ways families or even individuals spelt their names. It seems, however, that there may have been some clear distinction between those who spelt their name respectively Bolter or Boulter, as both spellings are used in contemporaneous entries in the church registers from the early seventeenth century onwards. This suggests the existence of two distinct families or different branches of the same family, wishing to be distinguished from one another for some reason. Even those who spelt their name in the same way might not have recognised mutual kinship and, within living memory, there were two such families of Bolters in the village. Even assuming that the name stemmed from a common trade plied by different families, it would be

188 One was in the photograph taken in that year.
189 Oral testimony to the author from Bill Phillips, who also provided a photograph of George Bolter in military uniform for the Millennium Exhibition of photographs in the village.

very surprising if two families with the same name in a village as small as Little Cheverell had no common ancestors, albeit remote in time – especially as, of all those named Bolter and Boulter in the United Kingdom, a very large percentage are traceable to Little Cheverell.[190]

Whatever the origin of their name, the Bolter family, who claimed a family connection with the highwayman mentioned above, made their mark not only for managing and staffing the brick works but as holders of the lease of Glebe and Greenlands Farms, as well as being churchwardens, hurdle makers, grocers, shop keepers and labourers – following in fact most of the traditional trades of the village. There was even one unfortunate listed as a pauper. Immediately before the Second World War there were three Bolter families living in the village. Ben Bolter lived at Beech Cottage, Bert and Les Bolter lived at Yew Tree Cottage and another Bolter family at one of a pair of cottages, now combined into one house, Meadow View Cottage.[191]

THE AXFORDS

The Axfords are another family whose name is no longer found in the village. Axford is a very ancient name in Wiltshire and one Adam de Axford appeared at the New Sarum Assise of 1333. By the late eighteenth century the family were well established as considerable tenant farmers in Little Cheverell and most of the tenantry land was by 1767 merged into a single farm, known as Axford's farm, of which Thomas Axford held the copyhold lease. (For more on Thomas Axford and his Commonplace Book see Appendix G.) The family's former prominence in the village is commemorated by an impressive memorial stone in the church above a family vault. The Axfords were also prominent in neighbouring places. In Erlestoke Isaac and Robert Axford were tenants of Peter Delme, the lord of the manor, whose black mare was stolen by the highwayman Thomas Boulter and, up until 1782, there was an Axford's Farm at Imber. Other Axfords were resident in Bratton.

THE PHILLIPSES

Bill Phillips, now in his late seventies, grew up, with his brother Reg

190 Memorandum on the Bolter family produced privately by Richard Bolter in 1998.
191 Now the home of Martin and Sarah Walker.

and two sisters Margery and Elsie, in Ivy Cottage where he still lives – the last resident member of a family established in Little Cheverell since at least 1700. His father Edward ('Ted') was, amongst other things, a 'lengthman' for the County Council, responsible for maintaining particular stretches of road, and his mother Bessie was the daughter of Samuel Smith, who, like his son Percy after him, worked for the Nosworthys as a shepherd. Bill's grandfather, William Phillips, lived at the west end of the village in No. 2 The Retreat, with their cousins of the Axford family living next door at No.1 The Retreat.

By the time Bill Phillips was of school age, the Little Cheverell school had long been closed and he, his two elder sisters and other children from the village walked across the fields to the school at Great Cheverell. Ken and Harry Edwards and two Axford boys were contemporaries there and they all left at the age of fourteen, which was then the age at which elementary education came to an end. In 1936 and 1937, when Bill was about eleven, he and three or four other boys used to earn a little pocket money as beaters for Robert Awdry's shoots on the downs above Hawkswell House. They worked under the supervision of the keeper, Charlie Jones, who then lived at Pillar Box Cottage and shoots were sometimes combined with those of the Holloways of West Lavington whose keeper, Jim Mundy, lived at the Warren below Strawberry Hill. The game in those days was mainly hare and partridge, with only a few pheasants.

Bill Phillips and George Bolter were boyhood friends and their two mothers were also very close to one another. Bill particularly remembers George Bolter coming home to say goodbye before being posted abroad during the Second World War when serving in the Royal Artillery. He had some premonition at the time, which proved sadly right, that he would never come back. Bill himself served in the RASC (Royal Army Service Corps) in Italy and elsewhere and, after the war, worked for most of his working life as a ganger on the former Great Western Railway region of the railways.

THE RIDOUTS

The Ridouts, well established in the village at least from the early nineteenth century, are yet another family with no male members still living in the village. The parish register of births shows a son, George, born to George and Mary Ridout in 1808 and a daughter, Charlotte, in 1811.

In the early twentieth century descendants of earlier Ridouts, Thomas with his wife Jane, lived in what is now known as Dinas Cottage, next to The Owl, where they brought up their seven children (four boys and three girls). The eldest, George, was among those killed in the First World War and Charles, who married 'Nell' Oram and lived in Great Cheverell, had two sons – Harry and Bert – and one daughter. The Ridout building firm was founded by the two brothers Harry, whose son Mervyn later took on the business, and Bert. A strong vein of musical talent ran in the family through several generations and the Ridouts contributed to local music in a number of ways. Harry's daughter Gill Wilding, for instance, became organist at Great Cheverell and Bert's daughters, Jean and Pam, organists at different times at Little Cheverell. On the business side, Harry's grandson Mark Wilding acquired Kyte's garage in Great Cheverell in the early 2000s.

THE SMITHS

The Smith family are remembered as builders, Harry Smith latterly being the head of the firm. They were also as a family remarkable for being good musicians and, in particular, providing the whole choir for the Baptist Chapel at Great Cheverell for two services every Sunday.

'HODDY' AND HIS GOATS

A name which still endures in Little Cheverell is that of a man who lived very much on his own.[192] He was not a Wiltshireman at all but a cockney, unfit for service in the First World War, sent to the country for his health. Ernest Hoddinnott, affectionately known as 'Hoddy', nevertheless left his mark on the village and the place where he lived in Low Road, now the home of Ian and Mary Wheeler, is known as Hoddinnott's Cottage.[193] His physical state apparently improved after his ulcers were cured by 'brown physic' which he called ''orrible'!

192 He had a son, Ben, who lived at one time in Nosworthy Cottage where the washplace was an Anderson air raid shelter (named after the minister who introduced them in the Second World War) – now in Mike Brain's garden. Ben Hoddinnott later kindly presented his father's embroidered milking smock to the village.

193 The house, now occupied by Mr and Mrs Ian Wheeler, was known as 'Raydee' in Hoddy's time and Miss Catherine Nosworthy, who owned it, named it 'Hoddinott's Cottage' in his memory before she sold it.

Even though he did not speak 'proper Wiltshire', he looked the complete countryman and was accepted as such. He enhanced the village's reputation by becoming an acknowledged expert on goats in the area and was a regular prize-winner, bedecked in an immaculate white coat, shining Army surplus boots and a cap, at the Frome Show at which Olive Awdry, widow of Robert, also showed prize goats.[194] He had an intense love for his goats and tended to wax lyrical about the shape and size of their udders. His billy-goat was stud goat for the district and he charged 'ten bob for a service but £1 if they drive up in a posh car'. People remember him bringing his grey dappled pony down to graze on Village Hall Field and his fame for administering a selection of secret herbal potions to sick animals was widespread.

'Hoddy' was more in the mould of the nineteenth century than the twentieth and his only concession to the twentieth century was a single tap of running mains water in his cottage. He lived 'without the electric and them modern things' and to the end of his days in the later 1970s never drank or smoked, and never visited a cinema. His simple philosophy was summed up by his dictum that 'Goat's milk don't give you tuberculosis and it cures eczema'. Having the courage of his own convictions, he imbibed liberal amounts of it himself.[195]

THE TAYLORS

The Taylor family, who became much involved in local affairs, lived in the village from the First World War onwards, arriving with Colonel Robert Awdry and his wife when they moved from Manningford Manor to Hawkswell House in the early 1920s. George Taylor had been Robert Awdry's chauffeur at Manningford but, called up early in the First World War, died at the age of only forty-six. This resulted in his son, Clement, taking over as chauffeur at the age of seventeen and moving to Little Cheverell with his mother Louise to live at Bridge House.[196] Clem Taylor and his wife, Dora, and family lived in the old school building after it was closed in 1922 and turned into a dwelling,

194 Information given to the author by Greta Taylor on 19 July 2004.
195 Article in *The Countryman* autumn edition 1981 by Commander John Manners.
196 Now owned by John and Jan Weyland.

appropriately called The Old School.[197] While Clem Taylor continued his employment as chauffeur, his brother Harry also worked for the Awdrys at Hawkswell and, later, the War Department. He and his wife Marjorie lived at Copsewood which later became the home of Freddie and Marjorie Child.

Clem and all the Taylors were regular worshippers at the church and much involved in supporting it. Harry was sexton and his duties involved looking after the large coke-fired fired stove, digging all the graves and winding the clock every week. Clem Taylor was also at one time parish clerk, in the days before the setting up of the parish council, and was popular for organising charabanc trips to the sea and elsewhere in the 1920s and 1930s. Louise Taylor was for a long while responsible for cleaning the church, a task Harry Taylor's wife, Marjorie, also took on at times.

Ken Taylor, Clement's son, retained happy memories of his home at the Old School, which he eventually inherited from his father. As Robert Awdry had provided piped water as well as electric light for tenants who were his employees, the house had a bathroom with hot and cold water. This was 'sheer luxury for ordinary cottages in those days when compared with the tin bath in front of the living room fire'. Nonetheless the copper for producing hot water was in an adjacent room and care was necessary to avoid drawing it all off and leaving an empty copper with a roaring fire underneath.

Ken Taylor had worked for Moore and Bush in Devizes and then joined the Fire Service, where Greta O'Neill whom he married in 1972 also worked. Much earlier in life they had known each other when she was at West Lavington elementary school before she went on to Devizes Grammar School and he, having passed the entrance exam, was at Dauntsey's School. At the West Lavington school Ken Taylor had a rival for Greta O'Neill's regard. This was Harold Beaven who, on his very first day there, cried when he was not allowed to sit next to her!

Greta Taylor's connection with village is considerably older than that of her late husband, for her grandmother, before her marriage, was Alice Mary Ridout, daughter of Thomas and Jane Ridout, who married an Irishman called O'Neill. Greta's father, Alfred James O'Neill, died relatively young and her mother Dorothy then married Douglas

197 The Schoolmistress's house was also turned into a house and is now owned by David and Jill Rowlands, among the longer-term residents of the village.

McGuinness. Greta Taylor, both in her husband's lifetime and afterwards, remained, with her long family connections in the village, active in both church and other local affairs.

THE WARNOCKS

Neither Joe nor Helena Warnock came from families long settled in the village. Nevertheless, like the Taylors, they made their respective marks and played prominent roles in local life from the 1960s onwards. Both were particularly closely involved with the parish council and the village hall committee.

Helena was living in Warwickshire when, in the summer of 1963 while on holiday in Devon, she met Joe Warnock whose first wife, Kathleen, had died in the previous year. He then lived at 4 Westbury Road, Little Cheverell and, although he later turned his hand to farming, was a mechanic working with Ian Kyte of Great Cheverell in Kyte's long-established garage there. For a few years he and Helena courted at long distance until deciding to marry. On hearing of this, Olive Awdry, the widow of Robert Awdry who then lived at East Sands, insisted in the late summer of 1966 on Joe bringing his intended wife to Wiltshire to see Pillar Box Cottage as a possible future home. This opportunity had arisen because her tenant, Charlie Jones the former keeper, wanted to move and she wanted to sell.

Before this could come about, however, there had to be a sort of 'vetting process' and Helena, after viewing the cottage, was taken by Joe to be introduced to Olive Awdry at East Sands, where she recalls the formalities of an age by then already fast disappearing. The door was opened by Lillian Mathews, the maid, wearing a black dress with a little white apron, which was the usual afternoon dress for maids at that time. She showed the pair into a room opening on to the garden, where agreement on the sale of the cottage was reached. The purchase was actually completed in November 1966 and, after their marriage in March 1967, Helena and Joe were able to move into Pillar Box Cottage.

'Great evenings' at The Owl are among Helena's happy memories of her early days in the village. It was then run by Ron and Rita Baker, who were both behind the bar every evening; at lunch time Rita ran it alone as Ron, like his father Percy, also worked at Manor Farm for John Wilfred Nosworthy. The Owl was then, she remembers, very much an unspoilt village pub, frequented mainly by locals. Local regulars included Les Bolter who lived at Yew Tree Cottage opposite The Owl, Ernie Wilkins, Bob Freeman who lived at Hawkeswell Lodge, Charlie and Polly Wheeler who lived at Fir Tree Cottage, John Seaborne from Erlestoke, Ken Watkins and John Walters from Great Cheverell, and Percy Baker, the publican's father, who at one time lived at Rook Trees Farm on Cheverell Hill. Unlike the public bar, the lounge bar was little used except by Dauntsey's boys who were not supposed to be there!

Helena's favourite drink was half a pint of 'scrumpy', rough cider with a dash of lemonade, costing only 6d. It was nevertheless strong and the only food available to complement it was a 'dodger', a small version of a cottage loaf with a lump of cheese and some raw sliced onion or packets of crisps with either a pickled egg or a jar of cockles. Although by then there was no village shop, Rita Baker kept a well-stocked freezer from which anyone could make some limited purchases.

The annual church bazaar took place, as it still does, on the last Saturday in November and was organised by Lady Crossley, one of the churchwardens. In her first year Helena was, as the wife of Joe, who assisted Joyce Crossley in a number of ways including jointly keeping a pig, asked if she would help. Even though she had never done anything of the sort before, she agreed; but wondered if her eyes were deceiving her when she first witnessed the length of the queue waiting outside the village hall long before the opening time. It even crossed her mind that 'she might be lynched pushing her way to the front of the queue' in order to take up her station at the white elephant stall.

All, however, went like clockwork and five minutes before the opening time Lady Crossley began a count down and then said, in military fashion, 'Stand by your stations' and finally 'Open the doors.' Two ladies at the front of the queue literally ran down the hall to the white elephant stall and immediately filled their bags with some of the wonderful bargains on offer, including silver and china. It was a time for many others to buy their Christmas presents too and business continued fast and furious at 'competitive' prices of a few pence (old money) for each item. Excellent nearly new clothes, some with expensive labels, changed hands rapidly and on one occasion Helena was involved in a family transaction between sisters-in-law when she sold a suit donated by Beryl Hanna to the rector's sister, Nancy Hanna.

Before the Warnocks bought Pillar Box Cottage, a public-spirited local milkman, living where David and Jill Rowlands now live, carried out a small service which helped the villagers considerably. Ray Coulson, who worked for Carter's Dairy in West Lavington and was affectionately known as 'Slug', collected medicine and pills prescribed for villagers from the chemist[198] in West Lavington and left them on a little bamboo table just inside the front door of Helena's cottage so that people could pick them up in their own time. Although that former practice ceased, a different version of the same principle still applies nearly forty years later, as people can collect their newspapers – delivered in bulk by Ian Smith of Great Cheverell Post Office – from a chair placed at the rear of Helena's cottage.

THE NIGHTINGALE FAMILY

Leathley Nightingale, who was director of music at Dauntsey's School from 1929 to1953, built East Sands, the white house on the east of the village now owned by Andrew and Anne Walker. In 1937 John Wilfred Nosworthy sold him half an acre of land, previously used as allotments and long known as East Sands, and the house, designed by the Devizes architect Gimson, was built by Maslens in the spring and summer of 1938. For his first eight years at Dauntsey's, to which he came from Monkton Combe, Leathley Nightingale and his bride, Joy Robinson, had, before deciding to build the new house, lived in rented accommodation at the Glebe House in West Lavington.

Their son Bruce later had a distinguished life in the British Council and wrote an autobiography, *Seven Rivers to Cross*, in which he gives some glimpses of his early life in Little Cheverell. He recalls climbing over the wooden scaffolding and watching the builders at work on East Sands, observing too the fencing of the property to separate it from the allotments which remained on the west side. More generally he remembers that the village was then, as now, a place of about 150 souls, all of whom the Nightingale family knew.

There were few facilities then, apart from a very small shop, regarded mainly as a source of sweets, and most people walked or bicycled to do their shopping elsewhere. Spares for bicycles were available

198 The chemist's was one of the three shops which stood where the minimarket now is.

at the Wheatsheaf Cycle Stores, which later became The Stage Post public house. The nearest butcher was at the Lavington crossroads and other shops in West Lavington included Pikes, the newsagents; Colemans, the grocers; and the post office. The blacksmith there shod horses at his premises close to the Manor House and petrol for the car was available at Holliday's garage, where it was dispensed by the hand-operated winding pumps common at that time. There were two local doctors in Littleton Panell and West Lavington – Dr Grey and a lady doctor, Dr Skene. People could get from West Lavington to Devizes quite easily by taking a bus, operated by the Bath Tramways Co., which ran hourly on the Bath to Salisbury route.

Bruce Nightingale clearly remembers the horses ploughing on Pocock's Farm, and receiving the reward of an apple at harvest time after a morning leading the wagon horses. He summed up his youthful impressions:

> At the time of my birth in 1932 the countryside was undisturbed; very occasional motor traffic, horses rather than tractors on the farms, elm trees, a working blacksmith in the West Lavington, bicycles quite popular, and regular congregations in the churches. The Army was in evidence during manoeuvres from time to time; otherwise contact with the world at large was restricted to travel by the steam trains of the Great Western Railway, either up to Paddington or to the West. The Cornish Riviera Express whistled through Lavington station once a day.

People who travelled without luggage normally walked to the station or went by bicycle, but he was taken there with his luggage in his parents' small car, when he went away as a small boy to school at St George's, Windsor, where he ended up as head chorister.[199]

The Nightingales' neighbours were the Beaven and Pocock families[200] and and there were social occasions with Catherine and Judith Nosworthy. The family obtained their fresh milk from the Beavens' smallholding and dresses for Bruce's sisters, Sheelagh, Jenny, Phillida,

199 He later gained a musical scholarship to Clifton College. Christopher Hawley, who lived at Little Cheverell House with his parents, also went to St George's, Windsor from 1982 to 1987 and ended up as head chorister and head boy, before gaining a musical scholarship to Radley College. He also played the trumpet in the National Youth Orchestra of Great Britain.

200 Harold Beaven has contributed his own recollections separately.

and Antonia, were made by Mrs Draper, who lived at the old School House. Another of Bruce's varied recollections is of trucks full of linen from Hawkswell and Little Cheverell House being taken along Low Road to and from Laundry Cottage where the laundry was done by two elderly spinsters.

Frank Beaven would use the Nightingales' telephone if he needed to call the vet and on one occasion he arrived complaining that one of his cows was suffering from 'oodendung' – it was not always easy to understand Frank Beaven's Wiltshire accent. It transpired, however, that this meant 'wooden tongue' and, as the vet would not be able to arrive for some time, Bruce's mother went over to the Beavens' farm, where the cow clearly had something down its throat. While the farmer held the animal's mouth open, Joy Nightingale reached down and pulled out the obstruction – thus gaining an unexpected local reputation as a veterinarian.

THE FLOODS

The manner in which Brigadier Bob Flood and his Jeannette transformed Cheverell Mill is a particular example of change in the village. The old mill and mill house had been owned by Jack Turner, who farmed the land around the house and kept a dairy herd there. By the later 1960s the buildings had been condemned as a dwelling but, when Bob[201] and Jeannette Flood heard this, they decided they would like to buy them. The owner's response to their approach, however, was surprising. 'You're not going to pay me for that,' said Jack Turner, 'I was going to have to knock 'er down.' Nevertheless a reasonable price was settled on and work on the conversion, begun in 1971, was finished in 1972. It was mainly carried out by a builder from Wootton Bassett, but the Floods also had great help from their neighbours, for Bert Ridout, the brother of Harry and uncle of Mervyn, helped considerably with the brickwork and Jack Turner himself kept an eye on things when they were away.

The mill property was turned into an attractive house surrounded by a beautiful garden, later opened to the public. Bob Flood himself had a degree in horticulture from Reading University and Jeannette was also an expert and energetic gardener. Together they transformed the garden

201 Brigadier Robert Flood, OBE.

area, assisted by several people living in the village, including Joyce Lady Crossley, who was a keen plantswoman. She donated some of her plants and cuttings and permitted her gardener at Little Cheverell House, Robert Mouland, to lend a hand where possible. Pat Patterson, Jack Turner's cowman, and both Jim and David Coxhead were also involved; and Jim began a new long connection with Cheverell Mill by becoming gardener to Brigadier Flood and later to Barny Beddow, who bought the Mill in the later 1990s. Mrs Patterson and Mrs Rhoda Whiting were also a great support to the Floods in the house itself.

Bob Flood played a prominent part in the village as a churchwarden and also as organiser of the National Gardens Scheme in Wiltshire as successor to Joyce Crossley. The gardens of Cheverell Mill as well as Little Cheverell House and of Hillier's Cottage, the creation of Marjorie Wort, were opened to the public once a year under the National Gardens Scheme for several years.

THE TWO WORLD WARS

The even tenor of village life was severely shaken by the two world wars of the twentieth century, which left their mark and scars on two or three generations and also caused or precipitated great social changes.

THE FIRST WORLD WAR

There is no record of the men who volunteered or were called up for military service in the Great War. It took a heavy toll, however, of the young men of Little Cheverell as elsewhere and the War Memorial, erected in 1921 in the north east corner of the churchyard, commemorates the ten village men killed:[202]

Albert Henry Belsey Amor	Royal Navy
William Copland Austin	Royal Scots
Charles Selwyn Awdry (eldest son of Charles Awdry)	Royal Wiltshire Yeomanry
Joseph Henry Bolter	Wiltshire Regiment
Archibald Henry Frederick Collins	Royal Wiltshire Yeomanry
Reginald Vere Collins	Wiltshire Regiment

202 Their names are also commemorated on a framed plaque hanging in the church.

Albert William Fidler	Wiltshire Regiment
George Henry Ridout	Royal Dublin Fusiliers
Evan Frank Sainsbury	Marine Gun Corps
William Henry Smith	Wiltshire Regiment

THE SECOND WORLD WAR

When the Second World War broke out, only twenty-one years after the end of the first, everyone was again affected. A number of men from the village joined the Armed Forces, either as volunteers or when 'called up'.[203] Mercifully the casualties were less than in the earlier war and George Bolter was the only Little Cheverell man killed on active service. Those known to have served were:

George Bolter, killed near Monte Cassino in Italy (Royal Artillery)
Jim Bolter (Royal Navy)
Joe Walter Bolter (Army)
Ken Edwards (Royal Marines)
Harry Edwards (Army)
Harold Goddard (Royal Navy)
Douglas William McGuiness, wounded in Sicily (Royal Marines)
Eileen McGuinness (WRNS)
Bill Phillips (Royal Army Service Corps)
Cyril Smith (Army)

Towards the end of the war, and after it, those called up under the Emergency Powers Defence Act of 1940 could be required to do duties other than military, including service with the National Coal Board. Those who had this experience included Ken Taylor, who was one of the 'Bevin Boys' – named after Ernest Bevin, Minister of Labour and National Service from 1940 to 1945 and later Foreign Secretary.

During 1938, the year before war actually broke out on 3 September 1939, preparations were made all over the country and two air raid wardens were appointed for the village, with Leonard Edwards of Marlen, the father of Ken Edwards, as head warden. He and Clem Taylor went to air raid precautions (ARP) training sessions and, as memories of gas warfare by both sides in the First World War were still

203 For National Service.

Stone Age tools found in north of village

Other Stone Age weapons and tools

Samuel Smith, a village shepherd, with his flock on Salisbury Plain

The sheep dip restored

Threshing, early 1900s

A feminine hand to the plough

Pre-First World War villagers involved with Little Cheverell Dairy after takeover by Wilts United Dairies Company Ltd. Dairy buildings now Bridge House and Pillar Box Cottage, with – further back – thatched barn now demolished.

Combine harvester driven by Clem Taylor. Ernie Wilkins on right. Manor Farm 1950s.

J. W. Nosworthy's employees – Percy Wilkins, George Cox, Percy Baker and Ernest Hoddinott ('Hoddy') – honoured with the Royal Agricultural Society's Long Service awards. Probably 1950s or 1960s.

'Hoddy', with one of his prize goats

J. W. Nosworthy's farm staff, 1973

Mrs J. W. Nosworthy and Miss Catherine Nosworthy with wives of the farm staff, 1973

Olive Cox, loyal church member, who was invited to a Buckingham Palace Garden Party. Wife of Bill, daughter-in-law of village's last shepherd, George Cox.

Village Hall Committee responsible for restoration of the sheep dip at opening ceremony, June 2004

LEFT Percy Wilkins with, behind, Glebe Farm House and farm buildings, now demolished – opposite church RIGHT Three boys evacuated from London in 1939 with Alan Roberts of Glebe Farm on right

Cheverell Scouts in 1940s with Percy Wilkins, Scoutmaster

General view of the brickworks

Delivery van from Mr Webb's West Lavington Bakery in Low Road with Ken Edwards and daughters Alison (left) and Sarah

Workers at Turner's Brick, Tile and Pipe Works in Little Cheverell, c. 1900

Little Cheverell football team, pre-First World War

C. H. WOODWARD, MACHINE PRINTER, DEVIZES.

From TURNER BROS.,
BRICK, TILE, & PIPE MANUFACTURERS,
COAL MERCHANTS, &c.,
LITTLE CHEVERELL.

Date April 27th 1907

600 Bricks

Tiles 4/2

Pipes

Coal

To Mr. H. W. Hooper

Delivered by own waggon

Invoice from Turner Bros. for bricks supplied, 1907

Workmen who built Hawkswell House about 1914

Low Road, postcard of early 1900s

Early 1900s postcard of Laundry Cottage in Low Road

Meadow View Cottage and Myrtle Cottage. Open land on right where Cedar Croft and Cold Harbour were built in the 1960s.

The Retreat on right and Meadow View on left. Early 1900s postcard.

LEFT Ken Taylor aged about five in front of drive of Little Cheverell House. Ford on right. RIGHT Greta Taylor aged about seven.

West Lavington British Legion (c. 1960), with four from Little Cheverell – Joe Warnock, fourth from right in right hand column, with Bill Phillips immediately behind him, Robert Mouland to his left and, extreme left behind, Reg Phillips

Wedding of Ted and Meta Wilkins; Ron Baker – the best man – on left,
Ernie Wilkins on right

Leonard and Mary Edwards with sons Ken and Harry and daughter Sue

Charles Turner and his family

Thomas and Jane Ridout with their seven children: l to r, back, George (killed in First World War), Alice McGuinness (Greta Taylor's grandmother), Fred, Lottie Cooper, Hedley; front, Bessie Smith, Thomas, Jane, Charlie (father of Harry and Bert, father of Pam and Jean)

Wedding of Albert Butler and Elsie Phillips. Behind bridal couple Bill Phillips, best man, with bridesmaid; behind them, Edward Phillips, the bride's father, and her sister Marjorie. Revd P. Sexty visible behind.

At The Owl when run by Ron and Rita Baker. Front: Ernie Wilkins, Hugh Whiting and Ted Drewitt; behind (right), Bob Freeman and John Walters.

Pre-First World War: from left, cottages demolished before Second World War, Glebe Farm House, elms all now lost and the church

A national occasion, possibly the Coronation of King George V, 1911

Thatched cottage, since demolished, known as Hargreaves Cottage and possibly earlier as Topp's Farm, to the north west of Pillar Box Cottage

Villagers gathered for celebration of the Coronation of King George V

The school 1904

Low Road with the school, the Schoolhouse, and Springside beyond

Schoolmistress and children 1922

Charabanc trip arranged by Clem Taylor (standing on right)

King George VI's Coronation (1937) decorations with Old School beyond

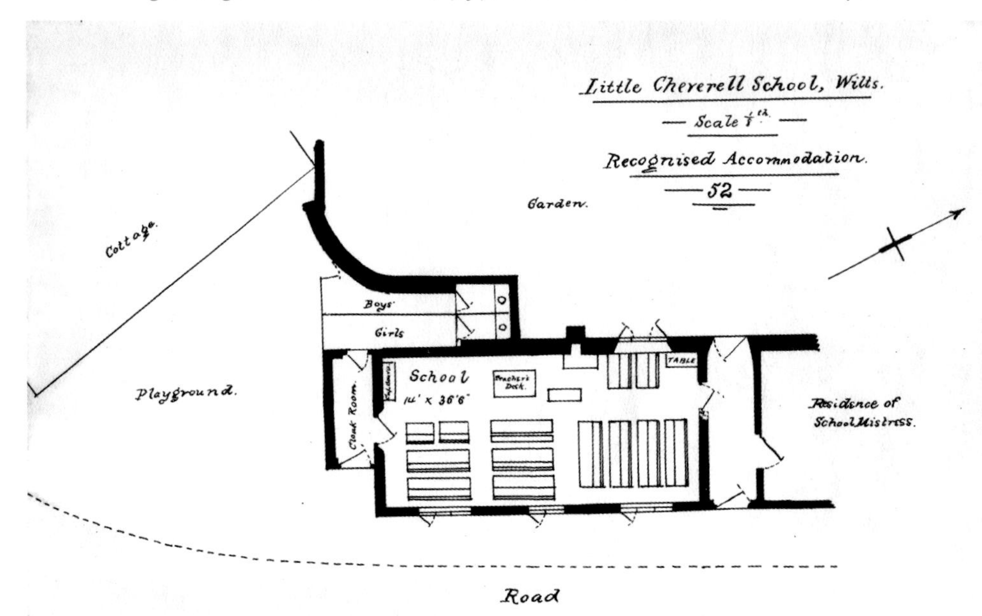

Ground plan of the former village school

Low Road – the same view as three pages previously (below), about 1950

Colonel Robert Awdry, High Sheriff of Wiltshire 1928/29

LEFT Admiral John Luce, CB, High Sheriff 1930/31 RIGHT The author's wife, Lady (Ruth) Hawley, High Sheriff 1998/99

WEDDING AT ST. PAUL'S

LEFT John Wilfred Nosworthy marries Madeline Robinson at St Paul's Church, Bath, 1927 RIGHT George Bolter, killed in the Second World War

Little Cheverell House, formerly the Rectory

Hawkswell House

Village Hall: fiftieth anniversary of VE Day in 1995

Village Hall interior: judging of Village Flower and Vegetable Show 2001

Opening of Millennium Green June 2000 by Catherine Nosworthy, who, with her sister Judith, donated the land. L to r: Mike Brain, Janet Weyland, Bill Palmer, Catherine Nosworthy, Helen Warnock, John Weyland, Victor King, Dawn Phillips.

East Sands

Furze Hill Farm, demolished c. 1960. Painting by Mr Grant-King of Laundry Cottage.

Former Rector's stables and coach house before incorporation into Cheverell Place.
Author in door of the hay loft.

Gathering at the author's Little Cheverell House in June of Millennium Year, 2000

Cheverell Place, first occupied September 2001

Cheverell Mill before conversion, early 1970s

Cheverell Mill, converted in the 1970s, photographed in 2007

Glebe Farm house

Pillar Box Cottage and Bridge House – formerly malt mill and then Little Cheverell dairy premises

Manor Farm about 1990

Littleton Panell Post Office about 1900

The Terrace

The Owl

St Peter's Church by J. Buckley 1807, before 1850s' restoration

Churchyard war memorial

The restored chamber organ

LEFT East window: Christ as 'good shepherd', central panel; St Peter and St John left; Isaiah and, probably, Jeremiah right RIGHT The church, early 2000s

Planting millennium yew, spring 2000. Parochial Church Council, l to r, standing: Dennis Alcock, author, Revd Terry Brighton, Linda Alcock, Eileen Ross, Victor King, Marlis Rawlins, Lynne Gammond, Spencer Gammond, Greta Taylor, Barny Beddow, Olive Cox, Ken Taylor. Front row: Betty Blackwell, Margaret King, Ruth Hawley, Peregrine Rawlins.

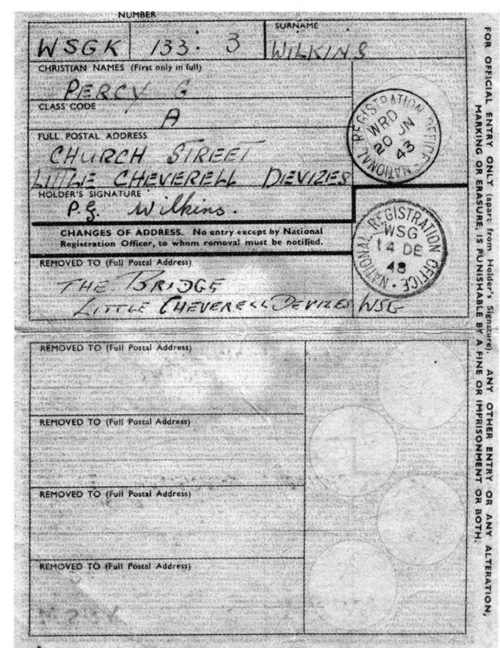

NUMBER
WSGK 133 · 3
SURNAME
WILKINS
CHRISTIAN NAMES (First only in full)
PERCY G
CLASS CODE
A
FULL POSTAL ADDRESS
CHURCH STREET
LITTLE CHEVERELL DEVIZES
HOLDER'S SIGNATURE
P.G. Wilkins.
CHANGES OF ADDRESS. No entry except by National Registration Officer, to whom removal must be notified.
REMOVED TO (Full Postal Address)
THE BRIDGE
LITTLE CHEVERELL DEVIZES WSG
REMOVED TO (Full Postal Address)
REMOVED TO (Full Postal Address)
REMOVED TO (Full Postal Address)
REMOVED TO (Full Postal Address)

NATIONAL REGISTRATION OFFICE WRD 20 JN 43
NATIONAL REGISTRATION OFFICE WSG 14 DE 48

FOR OFFICIAL ENTRY ONLY (apart from Holder's Signature) ANY OTHER ENTRY OR ANY ALTERATION, MARKING OR ERASURE, IS PUNISHABLE BY A FINE OR IMPRISONMENT OR BOTH.

LEFT Ken Edwards in wartime uniform as Royal Marine RIGHT 1943 identity card

Cheverells and Erlestoke Home Guard, 1941

fresh, gas masks were issued to everyone in the country.[204] Throughout the war itself, particularly in the early part, everybody kept their gas mask close by them in case of need, though fortunately no occasion to use them arose.

Once the war started there was a fire-watching rota and men walked through the village in the evenings to spot any type of fire, whether from an enemy incendiary bomb or as a breach of black-out regulations.[205] For some time a searchlight battery was placed in a field near Dauntsey's School and village lads spent hours watching the soldiers there sweeping the skies for German aircraft. The Local Defence Volunteers (later the Home Guard) were also active in keeping watch and training. When the LDV were first formed in 1940, they had little in the way of arms except pitchforks, but the Home Guard became increasingly well trained.[206]

The Lavington Home Guard's local headquarters was at the Wheatsheaf Inn in West Lavington and Leathley Nightingale, director of music at Dauntsey's School, who built East Sands and had been a Royal Naval Air Service pilot in the First World War, was one of those who joined this Home Guard. He also joined the Air Training Corps at Upavon and used his Austin 7 from time to time to take ammunition up on to Salisbury Plain for exercises. There was also a Great and Little Cheverell Home Guard, in which some men from the village served.

Civil defence exercises were held during the war from time to time and Bruce Nightingale recalls that, as a boy, he was called on to simulate a casualty near The Owl. After a thunderflash had been let off, a first aid party manoeuvred his limp body on to makeshift stretcher, made from a traditional hazel wattle hurdle, and he had a long and uncomfortable journey through the village as he acted his part.

Early in the summer of 1940 a twin-engined Junkers 88 of the German Luftwaffe, coming in low over Dauntsey's School, loosed two

204 The author was at school and, as a prefect then, remembers having to help younger boys fit and adjust their masks.
205 It was forbidden to show any light after dark and people often had to line their curtains with black material to prevent light escaping.
206 The author remembers joining the LDV when at Oxford University in May or June 1940. The members were issued with armbands marked LDV to give them military status if caught up in fighting German invaders. The Home Guard was better trained than *Dad's Army* might suggest!

bursts of machine-gun fire over the empty playing fields, before disappearing over Salisbury Plain. A 'shapely little Spitfire', the distinctive whistle from its Merlin engine sounding almost like the wind itself', pursued it and, so it transpired later, shot it down. The Spitfire pilot was Flying Officer Eric Marrs, a twenty-year-old former pupil of Dauntsey's who was naturally known to many of the boys still in the school, and his exploit not only caused pride and excitement but also acted as a strong spur to further Dauntseian recruitment to the RAF.[207]

Bombs also fell on Great Cheverell on 4 September 1940 and on Little Cheverell on 20 October 1940. Falling near the water works on the road to Erlestoke, the second bomb apparently put the water pump at the reservoir out of action and, as a result, the Nightingale family had to borrow milk churns from Frank Beaven to conserve water for a while.

Ken Taylor recalled a later attack:

> On 29th March 1941 at 9.45 p.m. I was cycling home from Dauntsey's when a plane dropped a Molotov Cocktail of thirty six incendiary bombs in fields behind Hawkswell, starting fires but otherwise no damage. The following evening I went up to these fields and found a large number of the bombs – some in pristine condition, others partly burnt and some completely burnt out. I returned home to collect a spade to extricate the bombs from the soft soil and retrieved half a dozen of them intact and they were taken home and placed in the stream for safety. They remained there until after the war, when the government requested that any such retrievals should be reported. The Army arrived to collect them a week or so after the police had been informed but left one solitary fin behind as evidence. A few other high explosive bombs were dropped locally in the Cheverell area but did little damage to either buildings or people.

As part of the 'war effort', local people not only participated in the Home Guard but also the Women's Voluntary Service (WVS), the National Savings campaign and the Vegetable Producers Association (VPA). The WVS had a jam-making operation at Hawkswell House, in which Mrs H. M. W. Robinson, mother of Joy Nightingale,[208]

207 *Air Crew* by Bruce Lewis, another Old Dauntseian. Eric Marrs, who was decorated with the Distinguished Flying Cross (DFC), was killed in the war and his name is amongst those commemorated on the Dauntsey's War Memorial.

208 Wife of Leathley and mother of Bruce Nightingale.

participated. This active lady was also the main local campaigner for National Savings, which involved stamps worth two shillings and sixpence (half a crown) being stuck into individual savers' books. The WVS were also involved in bottling fruit, putting down vegetables in salt and preserving eggs in isinglass. The VPA spread their vegetables and other produce for local sale in the garage, which was then part of the outbuildings of Little Cheverell House giving directly on to Sheep Drove opposite the Beavens' farmhouse.

Joy Nightingale became involved in 'salvage', which meant the collection of waste paper for recycling and of iron, steel and other metal utensils for melting down. She also kept nanny goats, served by a billy belonging to Mrs Rutter of Great Cheverell, and hens, ducks and rabbits. The customers who came to buy her eggs brought spare vegetable produce to feed these animals. Leathley Nightingale took up bee-keeping with some success.

Agriculture generally was harnessed to the war effort and John Wilfred Nosworthy played his part, for which he received a formal letter of thanks from Richard Stratton, Chairman of the War Agricultural Executive Committee, in August 1946. The letter included the words: 'Agriculture's share in the war effort played no small part in bringing us final victory, and the untiring work put in by members of Committees has been a most valuable contribution.'

Catherine Nosworthy[209] had a sad recollection about the First World War as well as memories of the Second. When she was a small girl, she saw large bones lying among the elms, which were still then a feature of the village, and was told that they were the bones of horses put down in 1914 by the Army and then boiled up for chicken food.

Her recollections of Manor House Farm in the Second World War include the very cool dairy, with its perforated zinc on the windows. Although it was no longer used as such, her mother used to make a small amount of butter and cheese for the family and to cure bacon there; and it was also where game and dead rabbits were hung. Rabbits were a good source of food in wartime, particularly as they were not among the rationed items. Many of them were therefore trapped for sale under Cheverell Cliff,[210] which was not afforested at that time but abounding in downland flowers and grass.

209 Memoirs of Catherine Nosworthy.
210 This was before the introduction of myxomatosis.

In the early days of the war, the WVS had to cope with a busload of evacuees from London on their way to safer places further west. They were mainly mothers and babies and a 'comfort stop' was set up in the village hall, where the Londoners were given food and supplied with clean 'nappies' improvised from old sheets contributed by people in the village. About eleven evacuee children spent a considerable time in Little Cheverell during the war and went with the other village children to school at Great Cheverell. One boy called Green had come accompanied by his father, who was a schoolteacher and joined the teaching staff at the Great Cheverell school for a while. Mr Green's appearance, however, caused some local comment, for he had 'black hair smarmed down with Brylcreem[211] and a small moustache', which was apparently a style then alien to the village.[212]

Virtually everything came to be rationed during the war, although fish, rabbits, sausages, offal and vegetables were among the exceptions, and everyone was issued with an identity card and a ration book, without both of which rationed goods could not be purchased from the shops. The requisite number of coupons, covering the particular items, also had to be surrendered when a purchase was made. This system lasted for some fifteen years and it was not until nearly nine years after the war that rationing came to an end under Winston Churchill's Conservative government on 2 July 1954.

Suspicion, as in the earlier war, about German spies and infiltrators was intense and Joy Nightingale remembers reporting that she had seen one or two torches or bicycle lamps being shone upwards from road bridges over the railway, which could have been potential targets for aircraft intent on cutting communications with the west. Such flashing was, of course, strictly forbidden at the time and, to make things more difficult for a German spy or an invader, all signposts were also taken down. Restored after the war, the Little Cheverell signs reappeared briefly as Cheverell Parva, which some people thought rather pretentious even though this usage sometimes still continues to this day.

VE Day, the end of the war in Europe, came on 9 May 1945 and was celebrated with flags put out on the houses all over the village. The Nightingales celebrated by not only draping a large flag on the front of

211 A creamy hair lotion, with a not very pleasant smell, much used in those days, particularly in town areas.
212 Ken Taylor's recollections.

East Sands, but erecting a temporary flagpole for another Union flag on the flat roof and flying the Blue Ensign.

THE FIFTIETH ANNIVERSARY OF VE DAY

An exhibition was arranged in the village hall in May 1995 to commemorate the fiftieth anniversary of the end of the war in Europe with the surrender of the German forces on 9 May 1945. Exhibits connected with the war were collected from members of the village and these included ration books, identity cards, petrol coupon books, government publications about air raid precautions, gas attacks etc, proclamations, magazines, uniforms, military insignia, commissions, certificates, gas masks and many other objects familiar to those who lived through that period.[213]

THE SIXTIETH ANNIVERSARY OF THE END OF THE WAR

Although some commemorative events for VE Day were held in parts of Britain, the Labour government of Tony Blair chose to change the pattern of previous celebrations of VE and VJ (Victory over Japan) Days by decreeing the week of 3–10 July between 9 May (VE Day) and 15 August (VJ Day) as a week of remembrance and commemoration. A well-attended 60th Anniversary Service was held in Salisbury Cathedral, but in the village there were no special events, although prayers of thanksgiving and remembrance were said in church services.

By 2006 only three or four people who had been on active service during the war remained in the village. Bill Phillips saw action in Italy and, after the war, was a loyal member of the West Lavington branch of the British Legion who always laid the wreath at the village war memorial on Remembrance Sunday. Peter Angell, who from 1982 lived in one of the apartments of Hawkswell House, served in theatres of war as far removed as the Russian and the Australian. He was a regular Royal Naval officer, who joined by special entry in the late 1930s and retired as a commander in 1960. He had a providential escape during the war for, when he was a sub-lieutenant on HMS *Hood*, he volunteered to serve in submarines and was transferred to that branch of the Navy; the *Hood* was sunk shortly afterwards, on 24 May 1941, by the German

213 This was inspired and largely executed by Wing Commander Victor King.

battleship *Bismarck*. The author was a captain in the Royal Artillery and served in the Middle East sector with Sudanese troops in the Sudan Defence Force. Eileen Ross taught in County Antrim, Northern Ireland, in a college where girls from Eire (Ireland), who had volunteered to join the Auxiliary Territorial Service (ATS) in the war, were given further education before joining units of the British Army.

VILLAGE CELEBRATIONS OF OTHER NATIONAL EVENTS: FORMER JUBILEES

Although no descriptions are known to have survived, old photographs show that Little Cheverell celebrated Royal Jubilees in the past with the same enthusiasm as other places in the country. There were many Union Jacks and much coloured bunting displayed for Queen Victoria's Diamond Jubilee and the Coronations of both George V in 1911 and George VI in 1937.

QUEEN ELIZABETH II'S CORONATION AND JUBILEES

The main events of the reign of Queen Elizabeth II are within living memory. Flags and bunting abounded for the Coronation in 1952 and for the Queen's Silver Jubilee in 1977, which was also celebrated by a large tea party in the village hall.

The Queen's Golden Jubilee celebrations in 2002, honouring the longest reign apart from Queen Victoria, were, in accordance with the Queen's own wish, in quieter vein than the Silver Jubilee of 1977. There was no village tea party as there had been for the earlier Jubilee but a celebratory concert took place, *inter alia*, in the church, given by the Swindon Male Voice Choir, the proceeds of which were devoted to the reglazing of the church windows as a combined Jubilee and Millennium project.

COMMEMORATION OF THE MILLENNIUM

2000, the year of the third millennium AD, the start of the twenty-first century, was celebrated locally in a number of ways. The Millennium Green, including a small garden planted with trees and shrubs, was instituted in Low Road with a large round commemorative device of black marble slightly shot red featuring a roebuck in the centre and a legend around the rim, reading: 'Cheverell Parva Lower Green. Donated by the Nosworthy family in commemoration of the Millennium 2000 AD.'

The opening ceremony was performed by Catherine Nosworthy who, with her sister Judith, the other daughter of John Wilfred Nosworthy, had given the land. The work on preparing the green had been done by the voluntary labour of individual residents, mainly members of the always active Village Hall Committee. Bill Palmer drew up the plan and supervised the broad landscaping which was carried out by a digger provided by Gaiger Bros., while Jan Weyland advised and carried out the planting of the garden. After the formal opening a 'Millennium' photograph was taken of the residents of the village, the great majority of whom had assembled for the occasion on the front lawn of Little Cheverell House, which was still then the home of the author and his wife.

A 'Millennium yew' provided through the local authority, and originally taken from a very old tree, was planted in the churchyard by the author as one of the churchwardens, in the presence of the Revd Terry Brighton and members of the congregation in the spring of 2000.

INSTITUTIONS: LITTLE CHEVERELL SCHOOL

The earliest known reference to schooling was in the late eighteenth century, when the poor wanted a school in the village itself, but there is no evidence that their wish was immediately granted. By 1808, however, a woman did keep a school there, although it had closed by 1818 and a fresh start had to be made in 1825 with a school for twenty-five children. A Church school, it was to flourish for about a hundred years and the rector was always very closely involved with it. It was therefore at the joint expense of the Revd John Fishlake and the lord of the manor, the Earl of Radnor, that new buildings for it were erected in 1849/50 close to the Rectory's main gate. The single storey school house had capacity for fifty-two children, while the schoolmistress – or schoolmistresses, as there were normally two in those days – was housed in the new house attached. It was a feature of country elementary schools in those days to have a large garden and Little Cheverell was no exception; it had considerable grounds behind.

According to a memorandum of 12 September 1914 in red ink in the minute book, a board of managers, two of whom had to be members of the Church of England and two appointees of the Education Authority, was responsible for administering the school. The chairman was appointed by the owner, the lord of the manor, who let the premises to the board for a peppercorn rent, and religious instruction had to be in accordance with the Prayer Book and the principles of the Church of England (Appendix H).

Until the Elementary Education Act of 1902, when the power to control secular education was transferred to the local authority, the school was managed and controlled by an independent board of managers. The board had to be reconstituted in 1903 with the rector, the Revd W. P. Nichols, as chairman and Messrs G. O. Pleydell-Bouverie, J. Nosworthy, J. Smith and A. Wilton as members. Miss Bouverie, who was formally thanked for her previous, unspecified, association with the school, was appointed 'correspondent' with the role of administrator and secretary responsible for entering into agreements with teachers and liaising with the Wiltshire County Council.[214]

Responsibility for funding also seems to have passed to the local authority as a result of the 1902 Act, for the meeting held on 26 March 1904 decided that the school house should be repaired and papered at Whitsuntide 'at the expense of the old Fund, the understanding being that the Managers would not be liable in the future for anything beyond the ordinary repairs done by cottagers'.[215] Greater precision generally seems also to have been called for at this time and it was decided that children under the age of five should not be admitted to the school and noted that the school had joined the Diocesan Voluntary Schools Association. The school-leaving age had been raised to fourteen by the Elementary Education Act 1900.

As regards others involved in the school, the Revd W. P. Nichols remained chairman until 1913, when his successor the Revd H. P. U. Margesson took over. In 1913 Helen Awdry, daughter of Charles Awdry and sister of Robert Awdry, became a foundation manager and thereafter seems to have played as prominent a role in the school's affairs as Miss Bouverie had done before her. Both, it is interesting to note, were close relations of the lord of the manor. In 1915 John Nosworthy, his wife and a Mrs Wilson were all praised for the 'excellent work for the children' they had done over many years.

214 Minutes of the school board in the possession of Mrs Greta Taylor.
215 This seems to imply that some additional help would still be available from parents and others for very small repairs.

Children always remember their teachers, but only a limited amount of information about those who taught in Little Cheverell is still known. For a while between 1840 and 1904 a Miss Bull was responsible single-handed for thirty to forty pupils of between four and thirteen years of age and she gained a reputation as a good teacher, who enabled 'many of the boys and girls to go out into the world to do well'.[216] In 1907 Miss Howse of Froxfield, with the agreement of the County Education Authority, replaced Miss Williams as headmistress and in 1909 Miss V. D. K. Sawyer replaced Miss Lancaster as 'supplementary teacher'. In 1912 Miss Howse resigned as head teacher and the managers placed on record their 'appreciation of the excellent manner in which she has discharged her duties'. Mrs Sarah Ann Edwards, her successor, to whom the school house was let on a monthly tenancy at a rental of £5 per annum, was appointed 'Certificated Head Teacher' at a salary of £12 per annum but she may have been less successful than some of her predecessors. At all events the managers noted the need in 1913 for encouraging her to obtain better results and, when she reached the age of sixty-five in 1915, the Education Authority was unwilling to extend her contract.

There were thirty-six pupils appearing in a school photograph of 1903/4, suggesting that the school was at one time in a very healthy state. In 1915 it was proposed, presumably in view of the retirement of Mrs Edwards, that the school should be closed until the end of the war and that the children should in the meantime attend the Littleton Panell school. This was not accepted and in 1916 Miss Archer was appointed head teacher, although from about 1918 onwards the school ran into increasing financial difficulties, perhaps through lack of provision by the local authority. By 1922 there were only sixteen pupils and a decision was taken to close it 'as part of the measures of economy which the County Council found it necessary to take'. From then on the children of Little Cheverell initially went either to the Littleton Panell school or, later, to Holy Trinity at Great Cheverell.

DAUNTSEY'S SCHOOL

Walter Pleydell-Bouverie, then living at Manor Farm in Little Cheverell, was involved in the 'revival' of Dauntsey's School at the end of the

216 Statement, unfortunately not dated but probably made in the 1950s, given apparently to ladies collecting for 'A History of the Village of Little Cheverell'.

nineteenth and early twentieth century and became the first chairman of governors in 1891. This school had originally been founded under the will of Alderman Dauntsey dated 1542 but by the second half of the nineteenth century had declined into a far from successful institution. The refounding only came about following very tortuous proceedings (and, strangely, much local ill will) but it emerged triumphantly as Dauntsey's Agricultural School with financial support from the Mercers' Company and the first meeting of the governors was held on 23 July 1891. Others living in the village were involved with Dauntsey's. Admiral John Luce was a governor; and, as earlier described, the house in the village closest to the school, East Sands, was built by Leathley Nightingale;[217] and Ken Taylor was amongst those who attended it in the mid-twentieth century.

Little Cheverell was mentioned in the memoirs of Canon Gillespy, one of the first boys in the 'new' school, who went there in 1895:

> We usually went to church on Sunday mornings and in the evening, if it was fine. We rang the changes between Market Lavington, Great and Little Cheverell and Erlestoke.... Little Cheverell Church lived up to its name; it was very small and so was the congregation. Most of the villagers present were very elderly[218] and could not read – I imagine – as they used no books, so that when the contingent from Dauntsey gave tongue in the hymns, the volume of praise was much increased.[219]

An eccentric farmer from Little Cheverell called Vosper also features in the recollections of both Canon Gillespy and his contemporary Frank Maggs, who later farmed locally. Vosper, according to the boys' account, appeared to be mad from delirium tremens, and frequently aroused terror by brandishing a large stick and yelling at them as he passed. A wonderful horseman, he would also gallop round shouting at night and ride recklessly down Cheverell Cliff, scaring Frank Maggs so much that he used to hide if he saw him coming.[220]

Canon Gillespy and Frank Maggs also noted that, in 1896, the Great Western Railway realigned their south-west route from Stert to

217 See above.
218 'Plus ça change!'
219 Jim Hodges, *A Conflict of Interests – The Origins of the Dauntsey Agricultural School and Its Early Years 1878–1899*, 1995.
220 *Ibid.*, pp. 57, 60.

Westbury, and part of the Dauntsey's boys' agricultural training involved assisting Mr Sainsbury of Littleton Panell to fell trees on part of his land, over which the new track would pass.

THE PARISH COUNCIL

A parish has from Anglo-Saxon times been an administrative unit, for both ecclesiastical and secular purposes, based on a town or area with a church and with defined boundaries. Knowledge of its boundaries was kept alive by the parishioners walking round the parish limits together once a year, and 'beating the bounds' was no doubt a custom followed in Little Cheverell. The parish clerk, whose office is coeval with the parish itself, was next to the clergy in status and originally his duties involved keeping the parish school, accompanying the priest when the visiting sick, and assisting in the services of the church. Nowadays the official with exactly the same title is an entirely secular office holder with very different duties.

The modern secular parish of Little Cheverell, administered by the parish council, remains coterminous with the ecclesiastical parish which is the responsibility of the parochial church council (PCC). This is a very faint reminder that, in former times, religious and secular responsibilities were not separate as they have been since the introduction of the Local Government Act of 1894.

The way in which Church and State were bound together before that is illustrated both by the former administration of the Poor Law and by the history of the 'vestry', a meeting originally held in the vestry of the church to transact parishioners' business. Parishioners meant all the inhabitants of the parish and not merely members of the church congregation.

Before state welfare benefits were introduced in the first half of the twentieth century, overseers[221] were appointed in every parish, as required by the Poor Law Act of 1601, to provide for the relief of paupers settled there. The necessary funds were raised by a poor rate, levied on property[222] within the parish. It was administered by churchwardens, who were *ex-officio* overseers until 1894, and, in some cases, other suitable men appointed by local JPs. Overseers were abolished by

221 An office first created by a statute of 1572 in the reign of Queen Elizabeth I.
222 Until 1862, only land was assessed for poor rate, but after that houses as well as land were assessed.

the Poor Relief Act 1925 and the whole Poor Law administration finally wound up by the National Assistance Act 1948.[223] Amongst overseers specifically mentioned in earlier times in Little Cheverell were E. Bazell, the tenant of Manor Farm, and Charles Turner, the owner of the brick works, for the year 1900 and John Nosworthy for 1918.[224]

The vestry meeting was – and remains theoretically to this day in Little Cheverell – an assembly of the whole parish. Its function is, however, nowadays much attenuated because the non-ecclesiastical functions were transferred in rural areas under the Local Government Acts of 1894 and 1933 to the parish meeting or parish council and the main ecclesiastical functions such as the election of churchwardens to parochial church councils established under the Parochial Church Councils (Powers) Measure 1921.

The modern form of parish council, created by the Local Government Act 1894, is elected periodically by those who have a right to vote under the Representation of the People Acts. The council, which must consist of at least five members, has powers to manage parish property, hold land and acquire it for recreational and other parish purposes; other powers include acting in the interests of the parish in connection with the village hall and allotments. They may also levy a precept on the district council for their funds. A parish meeting of all the local government electors must be held once every year. From the time of the foundation of the Devizes Rural District Council, Little Cheverell was within its jurisdiction and, when this ceased to exist, it fell within the purview of the Kennet District Council.

The 1894 Act provided that all parishes with a population of 300 or more would have an elected council and that parishes with a population of over 100 and under 300 could make a request for a parish council to the county council, which, however, was not bound to agree. Otherwise smaller parishes would only have a parish meeting.

The parish council of Little Cheverell, in its modern form, only came into being in 1973, created by the Wiltshire County Council, following a petition from the parish meeting on 27 April in that year. Great Cheverell on the other hand seems to have had its council in the new form much earlier.[225] After election of the five members, who included

223 Jowitt, *The Dictionary of English Law*.

224 Gillman's *Devizes Directories* of relevant years.

225 Ivor Slocombe, 'The Establishment of Parish Councils in Wiltshire', *Wiltshire Archaeological and Natural History Magazine*, vol. 98, 2005, p. 63.

Freddie Child and Joe Warnock, Michael (J. R. M.) Brierley – then living at Manor Farm – was appointed the first chairman at the inaugural meeting held on 21 June. Since then there have been seven other chairmen and six voluntary clerks (Appendix I).

Other elected parish councillors who played prominent and active roles at various times included Dennis Alcock, Barny Beddow, Peter Edwards, Sheila Edwards, Tim Davidson, Beryl Hanna, Mike Hardham, Bill Palmer, Robert Turner, Ian Wheeler and John Weyland.

MIKE BRAIN

One man merits special mention in relation to the parish council. He is Mike Brain, who, even if he does not speak 'proper Wiltshire', has lived as a bachelor in Little Cheverell since 1966 and was associated with the council from its very early days until 2002, becoming most active after retirement from his job as a Civil Service engineer in the Home Office in 1985. He acquired land from a developer, who, frustrated by the refusal of a planning application to erect six bungalows on it, was eager to sell it and he built his house, Coldharbour, there with his own hands.

The major contribution Mike Brain has made to village life during the last thirty years has been as unobtrusive as it has been positive. Very well informed about all aspects of Little Cheverell, he was not only chairman of the parish council from 1979 to 1983 but, after that, served consistently as clerk of the parish council for some seventeen years – from 1985 to 2002, when the inappropriately intrusive measures introduced by the Government of Tony Blair caused him, with many other loyal people involved in local government countrywide, to resign. His love of the village has inspired him to arrange historical exhibitions of village life. In addition, he has been a member of the village hall committee and was one of those who made the Millennium Green possible. A keen and skilful gardener, he has won many prizes in the village Flower and Vegetable Show, of which he has been one of the principal organisers.

THE VILLAGE HALL

The first known building for the village hall was a First World War hut erected, probably in the 1920s, on or very near the present site. The land was apparently formerly manorial but in 1968 it was conveyed by

Olive Awdry to trustees, one of whom was Joyce Crossley. From then on, the trustees were legally responsible for the management of the hall and the site. However, not much use was made of the hall at that stage and, at the instigation of Joe Warnock, a Village Hall Committee was started with the object of running it and encouraging people to use it. Although they are separate entities, there has always been a close relationship between the parish council and the administration of the village hall.

In the 1930s the hall was much used for village plays, dances and concerts, which provided local entertainment before the advent of television. Plays such as *Murder at the Red Barn* and *The Farmer's Wife* were staged in the 1930s. Mrs Sally Wilkins would play the piano or sing while others would recite in the Wiltshire dialect, do impressions and fill the evening with variety acts. For a number of years village children were invited to a Christmas party in the village hall and Ken Edwards recalls that Mrs Nosworthy and Mrs Awdry were the main organisers, while Miss Anstice Awdry (later Mrs Brown), Colonel Awdry's daughter, played the piano for games such as musical chairs.

During the Second World War the hall was used, as described above, as a reception centre for evacuees from London and subsequently it has been used not only for meetings of the parish council and the parish meeting but also for the parochial church council; the annual church bazaar on the last Saturday in November; the Harvest Festival supper; the annual village barbecue lunch; the annual flower and vegetable show organised by the village hall committee; special exhibitions of local interest; and other events arranged by organisations, to which the hall has been let.

THE WOMEN'S INSTITUTE (WI)

Little Cheverell no longer has a Women's Institute but, in its heyday in the 1930s and 1940s, it was one the bodies which used the village hall. For some while Little Cheverell took pride that its WI was founded and flourished before West Lavington even had one. Founded in 1930, it was the inspiration of Miss Edwards, a dynamic 'crippled' lady with 'piercing blue eyes' brought up in India, where unfortunately 'she had been left too long in the sun by a careless ayah'. After she moved to the village from Billericay she lived at Rest Harrow and her hallmarks were an ancient double-brimmed hat over her short white hair and a wheelchair, dependence on which seemed to fire rather than dampen her enthusiasm. Her energy led to her being at times both president and honorary secretary of the WI, in addition to which she was passionate about her garden and loved flowers and reading.[226]

THE VILLAGE DESIGN STATEMENT

'The Little Cheverell Village Design Statement' (VDS) was formally approved by the village and adopted in March 2004 as supplementary planning guidance for the interpretation of policies in the emerging Kennet Local Plan. Its broad aim is to conserve the character of the village and applications for planning consent under existing legislation need to show that due regard has been paid to this Statement. This document which contains valuable information about the village and its character was prepared by 'The Little Cheverell VDS Steering Team' with Andrew Walker as chairman, Michael Maxwell as treasurer and Bill Palmer as secretary.

LATTER DAY POLICING

Until about the 1970s most large villages had their own – always male – policemen or a single policeman. Although Little Cheverell was too small for this, Great Cheverell did have a resident policeman and Little Cheverell was policed either from there or from West Lavington. Nonetheless the local 'bobby', who was usually held in great respect and awe, was well known to villagers and very much part of the local scene.

The respect of former days is well illustrated by a childhood memory of Ken Edwards. The lack of traffic on Low Road in the 1930s gave him and his brother Harry confidence to take turns to use a wooden trolley to career down the bank opposite their house. One day Ken, then at the tender age of nine or so, came down the incline at speed only to collide at the bottom with the local policeman from West Lavington, who was serenely riding by on his bicycle on his village rounds. The juvenile Ken's brush with the pillar of the law, when they bit the dust together in a muddle on the ground, so alarmed him that, in those more

226 Manuscript in an unidentified hand and found with other records of the collection of information for the earlier 'Village History'.

innocent days, he asked his father: 'Dad, will I have to go to prison for that?' It took a little time to reassure him. Healthy fear of the law is also shown by the sense of slight disgrace felt when Harry Taylor in the 1940s[227] was caught riding his bicycle without a light for the short distance between Hawkswell House and his home at Copsewood. The policeman presented the case to the magistrates who fined Harry Taylor ten shillings.

When police codes and practice were rather more informal than nowadays, policemen habitually helped themselves to the cider in the barrel which Frank Beaven had on the go at harvest time in the 1930s and 1940s. On one occasion two policemen, arriving on their bicycles, indulged themselves so freely that, when they came to mount again, one fell heavily off on the opposite side. Beatrice Beaven, Frank's wife, saved the day by taking him home to Market Lavington in her Morris Minor.

COMMUNICATIONS: ROADS

The old Bath to Salisbury Road ran over Cheverell Down from Tinhead for a short distance at the extreme south of the parish. Other roads coming up from both Little and Great Cheverell are still to be seen meandering over the Plain. As menioned above, the hedgerows on either side still exist, though there are breaks, and in some places the road itself is clear with a hardcore of flints and edged with hawthorn, elder, briar roses, sloes, ash and the occasional wayside apple tree. Coaches, wagons, horses and riders were to be seen making their way 'up hill and down dale' as the road crossed the Plain. Before the railway era journeys were, of course, made on horseback, in a coach or wagon, or on foot.

For hundreds of years it was the responsibility of the parish to maintain roads, but the half-hearted observation of this obligation led to the introduction of the turnpike system in the eighteenth century. Specific Acts of Parliament were passed to grant companies the right to erect gates and toll bars in order to levy charges on users of a particular stretch of highway. In return the companies accepted an obligation to keep it in good condition. The Westbury to Market Lavington Road – now B3098 but then defined as running from 'Pengate (Parish of

227 Probable date.

Westbury) to Latchett's Bridge' at the east end of Market Lavington – was turned into such a road by virtue of an Act of Parliament in 1804.

There is evidence, however, that this road which traverses the village was already a turnpike road in the eighteenth century[228] and it seems that there was a toll house in Littleton Panell at the crossroads between the B3098 and the A360, and another at Bratton. Toll roads, however, became increasingly unpopular and the Littleton Panell toll house was actually burnt down. The final demise of the whole turnpike system was swift. In 1860 there were more than 1,000 turnpike roads in England, but by 1879 only about 200 remained. Locally the final abolition of toll gates was celebrated dramatically in November 1868 by a 'grand pyrotechnic display' at Devizes, attended by several thousand spectators.

By the 1930s maintenance of roads had become the responsibility of the local authority and the village's verges were, as mentioned above, tended by 'lengthmen' employed by the local rural district council – each responsible for his own designated 'length'. The neatness and tidiness of any stretch of road depended largely on the enthusiasm and dedication of one man and many took great pride in the 'length' for which he was responsible.[229]

VILLAGE FOOTPATHS

The pattern of footpaths, bridleways, tracks and roads has undoubtedly changed over the centuries but, for the most part, those habitually used in recent times have been recognised by the county council and marked accordingly both on maps and on the ground. Dr Tony Loveless, a distinguished but somewhat peppery retired scientist living at Dinas Cottage, took a particular interest in these local footpaths and was influential in the 1970s and 1980s in ensuring their preservation and marking by the local authority. Footpaths were his particular theme at annual parish meetings, which he attended assiduously.[230]

Some of the footpaths are particularly important for communication across fields where taking the road involves a much longer, and sometimes more dangerous, route. One vital footpath, gazetted by the

228 See above in connection with the final Inclosure Award of 1803.

229 Ken Taylor's reminiscences.

230 The minutes books up to 2002 were deposited with the records Office in Trowbridge by Mike Brain.

county council, runs from Low Road straight across the fields to Littleton Panell. Another one duly marked runs from Low Road, starting between Marlen and Copsewood, to the road connecting the B3098, near Manor Farm in Little Cheverell, to Great Cheverell. This was probably much used when the greater part of the local community living in Low Road went to and from work on the farm but, though marked on the map, it fell into almost complete disuse.

The reason was that another, unmarked, path – rather to the north of the marked path – had come to be used habitually since at least the beginning of the twentieth century, as it is the most direct route to Great Cheverell and neither landowner nor farmer objected. Many people had used it since childhood when they went to school in Great Cheverell and visited the shop. A new owner acquired the field in the late 1990s. The parish council then attempted to persuade the county council to declassify the virtually unused southerly path and, instead, to gazette the more northerly path as the public footpath, but this proved technically impossible. The owner created obstructions to the unmarked path and positions then hardened into a prolonged dispute, which gave rise to several public inquiries. The path was finally gazetted by the county council in April 2004.

BRIDLEWAYS

There are a number of bridleways. These include the path from Kit Farm to Littleton Panell, the private road known as Sheep Drove to the north of Cheverell Place owned by the riparian owners, and the private road from Orchard Acre to Low Road.

THE RAILWAY

The flowering of the railway system in the second half of the nineteenth century immediately opened up new vistas for many people. Until 1900 Devizes lay on the West of England main line itself, which took a more northerly route than it now does. The opening of the first station in Devizes in 1857 was celebrated by a twenty-three coach excursion to Weymouth on the Somerset and Weymouth line and one or two from the village were probably numbered among the 1,000 taking part. A line along a difficult route, including a 190-yard tunnel under Devizes Castle, had been engineered from Holt Junction, where the Berks and

Hants Railway and the Wilts and Somerset Railways met from 1862 onwards. It was therefore to Devizes station that, as mentioned above, the products of the Little Cheverell Dairy were taken in its heyday in the 1880s and 1890s. From 1900 onwards, Devizes ceased to be on the main line to the west, but was connected to it by a branch line to Patney.

The realignment of the main line in 1900 between Paddington and Exeter, via Reading and Westbury, brought it straight across the north of the parish. The new Lavington station, remembered subsequently by many servicemen in the two world wars as the place were they 'entrained' or 'detrained', made longer journeys more inviting for local people as it was within walking distance. Those walking to or from the station from the top end of the village would, weather permitting, use the track via Cathern Cross (Catherine Cross) turning left just before reaching the Lavington-Devizes Road and, via a path exiting on to the road opposite A' Becketts, at the top of what came to be known as Station Hill. Some people took their luggage to the station, pushing bicycles with a suitcase between the handlebars.

On weekdays in the 1940s and 1950s there were three daily express trains to London (Paddington) at 8.52 and 11.00 a.m. and an evening train at 6.17 p.m. In addition there were some trains stopping at all stations to Reading, from where there were easy connections for London – Paddington. In the opposite direction a train at 8.58 a.m. from Paddington to West Lavington offered connections to Weymouth and Salisbury with express services at 2.25 p.m. and 8.07 p.m. from Lavington to Weymouth. There was also a good rail service for parcels in those days and the small parcels office, which was situated on the down platform[231] would accept even the smallest. The office accommodated a writing desk and a sizeable solid fuel stove, which turned it into a welcome haven in bitter winter weather.[232]

However, Dr Beeching's purge in the early 1960s, when he was chairman of British Rail, put an end to all this and Lavington station was closed. Trains going by in both directions can still, however, be distinctly heard in the village, though it is frustrating that there is now no nearer stop than Westbury or Pewsey.

231 Formerly people spoke of 'going up' to London and 'going down' to the country. This therefore meant that the parcel office was on the platform for the line going towards Exeter.
232 Reminiscences of Ken Taylor.

BUSES

Before the Second World War Little Cheverell had a bus to Devizes on Saturday evenings at about 4.45 p.m. which enabled villagers to go to the first house 'pictures' – cinema – or for shopping before returning at around 8 p.m. On other occasions people walked either to Littleton Panell or Great Cheverell to catch a bus.

VILLAGE AMENITIES

There were few changes in village life in the short period of twenty-one years between the First and Second World Wars. Most of the amenities, now taken for granted, were lacking. The countryside was still unscarred by the power lines and telephone poles which are concomitant with modern progress. Fords instead of bridges were to be found on many country roads and horse transport was still common. No motorways existed.[233] The author recalls that in the first ten years of his life there were still horse-drawn cabs, wagons and carts in London and the motor buses, which had completely replaced the earlier horse-drawn buses, had solid tyres and were open on top, while the driver sat in the open without benefit of any glassed-in cab.

From 1945 onwards village amenities came with increasing rapidity.

HEALTH

There was no National Health Service before the Second World War, but hospital care was available in Devizes hospital and the parish of Little Cheverell joined the Hospital Saving Association in 1916 to enable this for a payment of £10 to the capital account and an annual contribution of £4.[234] Individual contributions were collected in the 1930s by Samuel Hobbs, then Admiral Luce's chauffeur, and, when he died, by Clem Taylor. The fifty contributors listed in the register[235] include one or two who appear to have been domestic staff living in Little Cheverell House.

Even when the National Health Service came into being after the

233 Author's own recollections.
234 Letter from O. Sheppard, Assistant Secretary of the Cottage Hospital, to John Nosworthy.
235 In the possession of Ken Taylor in 2000.

war, some people still resorted to traditional country remedies and Ken Taylor, who had earlier vainly put all available patent remedies from the chemists to the test, was among those cured of warts by Wally James, the son of the baker at Market Lavington with a gift for such acts.

WATER SUPPLY

It was not until the late 1950s, or early 1960s, that a public supply of water was available throughout the village. Before that, most people collected their drinking water in buckets from three 'dipping wells' or springs – one opposite Springside Cottage beneath the yews of Little Cheverell House, one close to Rose Cottage and the third by Marlen. Ken Edwards has memories of the 'dipping well' close to his home and of the nearby rail, on which people used sit and chat. Their cumulative weight made it increasingly concave. Little Cheverell House had, as old photographs and maps show, two tall wind pumps for raising water but even the occupiers of the few other houses which had wells or pumps often collected spring water for drinking.

Modern facilities reached the occupants of Hawkswell House earlier than others and a purpose-built tower there contained two large tanks, filled by electric pump from a well. This supplied piped water to the house and other buildings on the property, including Hawkswell Lodge. A piped supply also ran, through the stream in the Hall Field and under the road, to feed the houses mainly occupied by Robert Awdry's employees – in Pillar Box Cottage, Bridge House, The Old School, Old School House and Springside Cottage.

ELECTRICITY

The first house in the village to have an electricity supply was Hawkswell House, which had it from the time it was built. There was a battery plant, charged by a large Petter or Ruston Hornsby engine turning a dynamo, installed in an engine house in a small wood some distance from the house. This also provided the power for pumping water to tanks in the tower to feed the domestic water system. On 12 March 1934, however, Hawkswell House and the central part of the village nearest to it, including the Old School, were connected to the mains supply. It was not until 1951 that the whole village was endowed with this public supply and oil lamps and candles were still used.[236] No gas supply has yet reached the village.

TELEPHONE

Telephones had become nearly universal in the village by the1970s and 1980s and a red telephone box was installed by the Post Office opposite The Owl. In earlier times the few subscribers could not dial direct but had to make calls through the exchange in Devizes where an operator – often, like Pam Baker, female – had to be asked to obtain the desired number locally or, when further afield, to connect a 'trunk call'.

MAINS DRAINAGE

Before main drainage arrived in the village in the 1960s, lavatory facilities consisted of old-fashioned earth closets in the garden, although Little Cheverell House had its own septic tank systems and Hawkswell its own sewage plant.

POST

Before the Second World War, and for at least ten years after it, there was a post office in Littleton Panell on the corner between the B3098 and the A306 road to Salisbury. The village postman, Mr Hillier, lived in Hillier's Cottage[237] and, like other postmen living locally, made his several deliveries a day by bicycle. Ken Taylor particularly recalls Christmas Days, when the postman arrived carrying a bag full of letters and cards and wheeling his bicycle with the basket attached in front of the handle bars stacked high with parcels. Having delivered what he could, the postman had to return periodically to the Littleton Panell post office for another load. His compensation, however, was a liberal reward of mince pies and home-made wine pressed on him by the householders. Until relatively recently there was no delivery on Boxing

236 Recollections of Greta Taylor.

237 Later belonging to Mrs Marjorie Wort, who opened her gardens to the public there, and now in 2004 by her nephew Michael Maxwell (Recollections of Greta Taylor). Jim Wheeler of Great Cheverell Green succeeded Mr Hillier as postman.

Day, but postmen would come round to the houses to collect their 'Christmas boxes' – the annual 'tip'.

SHOP

Joseph Spiers is remembered both as the keeper of the village shop and local coal merchant, as well as being a smallholder before the Second World War. At a later stage there was a small shop associated with The Owl.

BAKERY

Although no one now living in the village can recollect a bakery in the village itself, there is an old baking oven at Hoddinott's Cottage. Bread for the village, however, was baked by Abraham Whiting at Cheverell Mill until 1914 and, in the 1930s and after the Second World War, Mr James, the baker at Market Lavington, delivered locally from a horse-drawn cart and later a van, assisted by his sons Wally and Eric. Bread was also made and sold by Hayters of Great Cheverell, who kept the shop and post office there. For many years now the nearest places to obtain a loaf have been West or Market Lavington.

MILK

Milk was delivered in the 1930s and up to the 1960s, before the modern obsession with health and safety regulations, by a member of the Beaven family with a large container hung on the handlebars of his bicycle. From this the customer could obtain a half pint, pint or quart of milk, straight from the cow and often still warm. Villagers are fortunate that the old custom of a milkman from one of the local dairies delivering bottled milk to the door still continues.

LAUNDRY

Occupied by Mrs Nurse in the 1980s and 1990s, Laundry Cottage was run as a laundry in the 1930s and 1940s by two sisters, the Misses Wilson, who provided all the clothes-washing facilities for the Awdry family at Hawkeswell, Little Cheverell House and also for the Manor House at Great Cheverell, then occupied by Mrs Bateson.

Laundry baskets were regularly transported to and from these houses on four-wheeled trolleys, sometimes by Ken Edwards. The laundry also did washing for the Holloways of the Manor House at West Lavington, from where the baskets were brought over and collected by car.

WASTE

In the days before plastic wrapping and supermarket shopping, domestic waste was minimal compared with today's. Cash in people's pockets was limited, credit facilities virtually non-existent, and parcels were wrapped in brown paper tied, if necessary, with string, while paper bags were provided for items bought in shops. Sweet papers and chips packets were not cast away with the abandon that they now are, although some still living remember that waste was liable to be deposited sometimes in the Hawkswell stream. Vegetable waste, gathered by indidivual households, was used for pig swill and old clothes were more often handed on down the line in all families than thrown out, although there were rag and bone men who made collections from time to time. The life of garments would be extended by women sewing and patching their husbands' and children's clothes and darning the family socks. 'Shop till you drop' would have been a very shocking concept to former generations.[238]

SOCIAL LIFE: THE PUB

'The Owl' public house, which has remained a central feature of village life, has at various times been an ale house and at others an off-licence. Its name has fluctuated between 'The Owl' as it was known in 1914 and 'The Gardeners Arms'[239] in 1933, only to revert to 'The Owl' again shortly afterwards. The first inn sign that local people can remember was very simple – an owl cut out of plywood and painted black. Before the Second World War it was only an off-licence and, although a pint of beer could be bought there, it had to be taken outside and drinkers usually sat on the bank opposite to enjoy it. During the 1930s when Mr and Mrs Martin were the innkeepers, they also ran a small village shop,

238 Personal recollection of several people including the author.
239 The Hospital Scheme records show that it was called this in 1933.

but it was perhaps the complications of wartime rationing which made it difficult to sustain.

RECREATION

Church feast days were probably celebrated in earlier, pre-Reformation, times with festivities, dancing and perhaps performances, sometimes with religious themes, by mummers and players. More certain information is available about village recreations from the nineteenth century onwards and the important place of the village hall as a centre for social life has already been mentioned. There was, of course, no television until the 1950s and visits to the nearest cinema in Devizes were confined to Saturdays, when the weekly bus ran.

Otherwise there was at one time a troop of Boy Scouts in the village but other children's pleasures were simple and included whipping tops, hopscotch, picnics and playing in trees. The ponds, which are believed to have been made by the Long family when they lived in the village in the seventeenth century, were a constant source of pleasure to young and old for bathing, fishing and, in winter, skating. On Sunday evenings in summer, villagers and their families were to be seen on the local hills, such as Fore Hill leading up to Salisbury Plain, taking pleasure in bee and other varieties of orchid, cowslips and other wild flowers.[240] Sometimes people also liked to go further afield and, between the wars, the occasional trips to the seaside in a charabanc[241] arranged by Clem Taylor were popular.

There were some limited sporting activities for some to enjoy and, when Walter Pleydell-Bouverie lived at Manor Farm House in the 1880s and 1890s, he organised sports on Easter Mondays which were very popular. A Little Cheverell football team also once existed, although it is now many years since the village fielded one. An old photograph of it is not dated but, judging by the dress, it seems to have been before the First World War. Another game once was the rudimentary cricket played by village lads before the Second World War on the road opposite the Old School. It was no fine cricket pitch but there was very little traffic on the now busy B3098 in a period

240 Ken Taylor's reminiscences.

241 The word may be nearly obsolete but it was the contemporary equivalent of a coach.

when only the best-off could afford cars, and the nearest vehicle might be a car being washed in the ford on the Hawkswell stream nearby.[242]

CONCLUSION

During the course of fifty years, from say 1950 to the early 2000s, the village has changed from one almost entirely dependent on agriculture and village crafts to one where farms remain but those working on them have shrunk to fewer than a handful. The number of families who have spent all their lives and whose forebears came from the village has, like farming, greatly diminished. Virtually all the houses are now occupied by those working from home, retired people and professionals, and others working in neighbouring towns or even in London. Nevertheless, and despite changes over the centuries, Little Cheverell, surrounded as it still is by open agricultural lands, has retained its essential character, integrity, shape and environment over the whole of a very long period.

242 Ken Taylor's reminiscences.

APPENDIX A

Inhabitants of the Village in Late 1930s and 1940s

The earliest easily available list of inhabitants dates from 1722[243] and other listings of houses and people are to be found both in *Gillman's Almanack* and *Fletcher's Directory* for a number of later years.[244] The personal recollections of people still living, however, perhaps give a better impression of the community and their occupations when the great majority still depended on farming in the 1930s and 1940s:[245]

1000 Westbury Road	Eddie Green (foreman to J. W. Nosworthy) of Manor Farm and his son Tommy.
999 Westbury Road	George Cox (shepherd) and his son Bill, who married Olive Page.
8 Westbury Road	Mr Phillips (postman) or Billy Isaacs[246] (bricklayer).
7 Westbury Road	Mr and Mrs Wicks at one time and then the Clifford family (probably both working for J. W. Nosworthy) .
6 Westbury Road	Nelson Brown (farm hand) and his son Dennis and daughter.
5 Westbury Road	Bob Phillips (farm hand), his son Clarence and daughters Audrey and Vivienne.
Manor Farm House	Mr and Mrs J. W. Nosworthy and their daughters Judith and Catherine.

243 490, 184 County archives at Trowbridge.
244 Among those held in Devizes Museum and editions for the years 1900, 1920, 1928, 1938, 1957, 1961 and 1966.
245 Those who contributed to this section, including Greta Taylor and Harold Beaven, cannot remember every detail and cannot guarantee that every name and fact is accurate. It is, however, unlikely to be far wrong.
246 Greta Taylor has no recollection of a Mr Phillips living there, although that is right according to Harold Beaven's memory. Perhaps both those mentioned lived there at different times.

Old cottages (now demolished) behind present Manor House cottages	William Goddard (dairyman) and his son Harold who married June Uzzell of Great Great Cheverell. There was also a 'Land Girl', Olive Dunning.
	Ernest and Mrs Kitty Wilkins (head cowman) with sons Percy (remembered for always wearing wellingtons and therefore sometimes known as 'The Duke of Wellington'), Ernie and Ben.
Glebe Farm House	Lived in by the Platt family in the 1920s. A Platt boy was one of the last pupils in the Little Cheverell School before it closed, and appears in the 1921 school photograph. He later became a Church of England clergyman. Later let to other tenants.
Barn opposite Church	Used for calf rearing by Ted Wilkins.
Thatched Cottage (now demolished)	Ed Hargraves (head carter) and his mother and sister, Win.
Pillar Box Cottage	Charles Jones (gamekeeper) with three daughters Millie, Gladys and Marjorie (known as 'Jim').
Bridge House	Mrs Louisa Taylor, mother of Clem, Harry, Ted and May.
The Old School	Clem Taylor (Col. Awdry's chauffeur and later tractor driver for J. W. Nosworthy).
The Old School House	Mr & Mrs Bert Draper (probably farm worker)
Springside Cottage	Robert ('Moulie') and Mrs (Mary) Mouland (Dr Newton Dunn's, and later Lady Crossley's gardener).
The Grey House	Samuel George Hobbs, Admiral Luce's ex-steward in the Royal Navy who became his chauffeur.
Dinas Cottage	Mr and Mrs Hedley (and Rose) Ridout (WD Devizes).
The Owl	Mr & Mrs Martin (licensee and proprietor of a shop at right end of building).
Fir Tree Cottage	Charlie Wheeler (railwayman – related to the Turners).
Beech Cottage	Ben Bolter (possibly retired at the time).

Yew Tree Cottage	Bert Bolter (worked for J. W. Nosworthy).
1 The Terrace	Mrs Wheeler and daughter Edie, and son-in-law Percy (Mr and Mrs Percy Phillips).
2 The Terrace	Mr and Mrs William McGuinness (worked for Hinksmans, coal merchants in Devizes).
3 The Terrace	Lillian Matthews (worked for Mrs Awdry at East Sands).
4 The Terrace	Miss Norman (had previously run the Stage Post, later Wheatsheaf, at West Lavington with her brother).
3 Ivy Terrace (now Ivy Cottages)	Lewis Draper (farm hand) – related to the Drapers mentioned above.
2 Ivy Terrace	Ted Phillips and wife with two sons (Reg and Bill and two daughters (Marjorie and Elsie).
Myrtle Cottage	Mr and Mrs Harry Smith and two sons, Cyril and Gordon (builders).
Yew Cottage (now Holly Cottage)	Eva Collins.
Meadow View Cottage	Aubrey Wilkins and son Ted (worked for J. W. Nosworthy).
Raydee (now Hoddinott's) Cottage)	Ernest Hoddinott (small farmer, known particularly for his goats).
Marlen	Leonard Edwards, two sons, Harry and Ken, and daughter, Marion.
Copsewood	Harry and Marjorie Taylor and daughter, Margaret.
The Old Laundry	The Misses Wilson (they ran the laundry, mainly for Hawkswell House, Little Cheverell House, and the Old Rectory, Great Cheverell).
Hillier's Cottage (now Hillier's Cottage)	Mr and Mrs Hillier (postman).
Meadow View	Leonard Ladd (cowman with Fred Turner and later J. W. Nosworthy).
Hillside	Mr and Mrs Fred Turner (farmer).
Furze Hill Farm (since demolished)	Frank Turner[247] (farmer).

247 Fred and Frank Turner were cousins.

Brick works (since demolished)	Then owned by W. E. Chivers (earlier by the Bolters and Turners successively).
Oakfield (north of Great Cheverell to Devizes road)	Will Turner, brother of Fred (farmer).

APPENDIX B

Names of Features of the Village

In earlier times, when people seldom went far from the village, names of local features were more in use than they are today. Such names used within living memory include:

(The) Allotments	Land used by villagers (adjacent to East Sands).
Bazell's (Basil's) Barn and Pond	Old Barn and Dewpond at the top of Cheverell Hill (formerly accessed by Fitch's Lane). Named after Edmund Bazell, a former tenant of Glebe Farm.
Bolter's Barn	The same barn as Bazell's but much more frequently known as Bolter's.
Bottom Farm	Farm in the valley to the south of Fore Hill.
Cathern (Catherine) Cross	Farm crossroads roughly half way between South View (Kit Farm) and Littleton Panell. (It is reasonable to speculate that this may refer to a cross situated there – perhaps dedicated, before the Reformation, to Saint Catherine.)
Cheverell Cliff	The rising land, now covered with trees but formerly bare, leading up to Fore Hill on the high ground above.
(The) Clay – or Big Clay	Fields behind council houses to base of hills to the south. Presumably the field once known as the Great Clay.
(The) Dene	Continuation of land from The Owl Inn behind Myrtle Cottage and the Hangings as far as a footpath by side of The Retreat.
Fitch's Lane	Former lane by Hawkswell Lodge (named after Mr Fitch, Col. Awdry's coachman, who died in 1967). Believed to have been formerly a right of way which was suppressed by the WD along with other rights of way after they had acquired the land.

Fore Hill	Formerly cultivated land above Cheverell Cliff and lying between Three Cornered Wood (see below) and White Road.
Furze Hill ('Fuzzell')	High Ground to east of village in Low Road roughly above the Retreat – at one time profusely covered with gorse.
Furze Hill Farm	A small farm including the high ground with house to the south of the Great Cheverell to Potterne road. (Originally held on lease from the rector but probably freehold after the sale of Glebe Farm lands in 1915.)
Garston	Place on the edge of Great Cheverell but has come to denote the road leading there from Manor Farm Cottages to Great Cheverell. In recent years this has been signposted as 'School Lane'.
Glebe Farm	Also known as Parsonage Farm, based on the farm house situated close to Manor Farm House.
Greenlands Farm	A farm with farm house at the extreme north of the village, at one time held on lease from the lord of the manor and at times farmed with Manor Farm.
(The) Green	Area on the borders of Great Cheverell, immediately north-west of the Great Cheverell to Potterne road.
Green Road	Road from Planks Gate on Westbury Road (see below) to Bolter's (Bazell's) Barn and former dew pond.
(The) Hangings	High Ground on opposite side of road from Hoddinott's Cottage – used for keeping goats.
Hatter's Orchard	An orchard, the site of which remains unidentified, though mentioned in eighteenth-century manorial records. Possibly the orchard to the north of the former Rectory, part of which is now called 'Orchard Acre'.
(The) Hollow	Section of road between the Wilderness (see below) and the grounds of Little Cheverell House.

(The) Horses' Field	Field between Hawkswell House and the Churchyard – so called because almost all the Nosworthys' horses were kept in this field when not in stables. Used by youths of the village for football and for congregating with cycles etc.
Jericho Clump	An unidentified clump of trees mentioned by John Wilfred Nosworthy – probably no longer standing.
(The) Lane	Lane leading round the periphery of the grounds of Cheverell Place (formerly Little Cheverell House) from The Owl Inn to the B3098.
The Lynches	Narrow flat piece of grassland at base of hill between Bazell's Barn and Three Cornered Wood.
(The) Market Place	The road outside The Owl Inn (close to the present phone box) – presumably where a small market for goods was once held.[248]
Manor Farm	Originally the farm of the lord of the manor's demesne, known as Demesne Farm and later Little Cheverell Farm as well as Manor Farm. Always the largest and most significant farm in the village throughout history, it sometimes included some of the smaller farms.
New Zealand Farm	A farm with house lying to the south of the old Bath-Salisbury slow coach road at the south of the parish, so-called because of its perceived distance in the nineteenth century from the heart of the village. It was part of the manorial farmlands.
Parsonage Farm	See Glebe Farm above.
Planks Gate	Start of Green Road on Lavington to Westbury Road next to Dauntsey's School (between East Sands and Dauntsey's). Possibly one of the Planke or Plank family mentioned in church and manorial records may have

248 Reminiscences of Ken and Greta Taylor.

	placed a gate there at some time. Plank is still a name found in the area, though not in the village. (This feature is just beyond the parish boundary.)
(The) Piece	Field behind Manor Farm House down to Shovel Wood (ideal for tobogganing after snowfall).
Piggery or Piggeries	Location to the south of the last houses on leaving the village to the west towards Erlestoke – known as 'Piggery Cottages'. Pigs were kept in styes there when Walter Pleydell-Bouverie farmed Manor Farm personally, and the pigs were fed on the whey and skim milk from Little Cheverell Dairy.
(The) Ram	Hydraulic water raising and lifting machine beyond Hawkswell Engine House and Battery House.
(The) Retreat	Two semi-detached houses on Low Road to the north of the village below the high ground to the east.
(The) Rings	Field opposite Manor Farm main entrance formerly containing three rings of sweet chest-nut trees.
Roller House (and Roller House Hill)	Field immediately before council houses (adja cent to Lavington to Westbury Road) and incline on road up to it. Said by one villager to have been called this as whenever roads were being repaired in the vicinity the steamrollers and associated caravan and water barrels etc were always parked in this field. In earlier days the steamroller drivers lived on site as their base would have been some distance away.
Shovel (or Shovell) Wood	So-called, according to old villagers, because it is shaped like a shovel – between rear of Copsewood in Low Road and Garston. Also know as Cheverell Copse.
South View Farm	A small farm, farmed by Frank Beaven originally on lease as part of the rector's glebe

	lands but bought by him after the glebe lands were sold in 1915.
Three Cornered Wood	Wood on side of Hill between Bolter's/ Bazell's Barn and White Road.
Village Hall Field	Now called the Village Green.
White Road	Chalk road from Westbury Road to Hill Bottom Farm (now hard surfaced and gated).
The Wilderness	High bank from Fitch's Lane.
Withy Bed	Land in a dip of The Rings field – presumably where willow wands and osiers were once gathered.

APPENDIX C

St Nicholas of Myra

This saint, born in Patara on the southern coast of Asiatic Turkey in about AD 260, was Bishop of nearby Myra. He participated in 325 in the Council of Nicaea, at which the Nicaean Creed was established, and died in 350. Famous both for his generosity and – like many other saints – miracles, he became the patron saint of sailors as well as children. The origin of the Christmas stocking is said by some to be that St Nicholas, 'Santa Claus', wanting his charity to be anonymous, dropped some coins down the chimney of the house of two girls in Myra, whose family had become impoverished, and that by chance these coins fell into their stockings hung up to dry in the grate. The anonymous bonanza enabled them to get married, which otherwise they would not have been able to do.

St Nicholas's relics were probably originally held in a church on the island of Gemiler – St Nicholas Island, not far from his birthplace – and a major pilgrimage was established there in the sixth century. He was also much revered in both in the Orthodox Church of Byzantium and the Russian Orthodox Church, after the Russians were converted to Christianity by Prince Vladimir of Kiev (956–1015). It was because of 'St Niklaus' that Nicholas became a favourite name even with the Czars, including the last ill-fated one who was murdered at Ekaterinburg by the Russian Communists in 1918. Five Popes took the name of Nicholas between the ninth and fifteenth centuries and in the twentieth century St Nicholas inspired the composer Benjamin Britten to write an oratorio about his life.

The cult of Saint Nicholas spread from the southern coast of Turkey to Bari in southern Italy, where his relics were placed in the cathedral by Italian sailors in the eleventh century. For this reason he is often known as St Nicholas of Bari. His cult however spread northwards, reaching Britain, and for some centuries he ranked number three – after the Virgin Mary and All Saints – among those to whom churches were dedicated.[249] At the time relics of saints were much prized in monasteries and churches,

249 Information given to the author by the Bishop of Salisbury, the Rt Revd David Stancliffe, on 5 December 2004.

as the second Council of Nicaea in 787 had insisted on the use of relics in the consecration of new churches, decreeing that any church which had been consecrated without them should acquire some as soon as possible.[250] In every part of Europe churches announced with pride that they had acquired part of St Nicholas's body. It is conceivable, therefore, that some such claim – odd as it may strike twenty-first century people – was made in Little Cheverell when the church was originally dedicated to this saint.[251]

250 Jonathan Sumption, *Pilgrimage*, pp. 29, 34, 36 and 37.
251 The reverence of relics is not confined to the Christian Church. Buddhist temples – such as the Temple of the Tooth in Kandy in Sri Lanka – hold relics attributed to the Buddha, and across North Africa there are countless small tombs raised to commemorate local holy men, often containing their bones.

APPENDIX D

Local Press Report on Re-Dedication of the Church 1850

'The church was reopened for Divine Service on Tuesday 19th November. This small church had been reduced by time and mismanagement to a state of such entire decay that it had become necessary to rebuild from its foundations the whole edifice except the tower. The Rector, assisted by the liberality of the Earl of Radnor[252] and a considerable parish rate, has succeeded in completing a simple and substantial building adequate to the needs of the parish. The style of the architecture is that of the 14th century; and in the chaste simplicity of the work generally and the decent order and arrangement of the details (solid without ornament) this little church stands forward[253] as an additional instance of the progress of the church architecture in this diocese.

'The work has been finished in a very creditable manner by Messrs. Bilton and Sainsbury of West Lavington under the direction of Messrs. Cundy of London at an outlay of £500, exclusive of timber given by the Earl of Radnor. That a parish church has been built for comparatively so small a sum will, we trust, be an encouragement to other parishes, where similar restorations are required.

'On this occasion the morning prayers were read by the Rector, assisted by his Curate, the Rev. C. Cream, and the evening prayers by the Rev. M.W. Mayow, Rural Dean. A very admirable sermon was preached in the morning by the Rev. Prebendary Crawley, Vicar of Steeple Ashton from 2nd Chronicles chap.13, in the course of which the preacher most appropriately pointed out from Exodus chap.30, 12–16 and Nehemiah 10.32 compared with Deuteronomy 16.16 that the present legal responsibility of landholders to repair their parish churches, aided by voluntary contributions, is an exact counterpart of the Mosaic law. The Sermon in the evening was preached by the Rev. James Fraser, Rector of Cholderton, from Psalm 96 v. 9, in which he enlarged in

252 Then lord of the manor.
253 *Sic.*

eloquent language on the growing feeling of the present day in making the Houses of God in some measure corresponding with the high and holy purposes for which they are designed – at the same time reminding his auditors that though the majesty of God does require that He be worshipped "in the beauty of holiness" it is yet far more essential that the hearts of the worshippers should be awed by his holy name and that he should be worshipped in spirit and in truth.

'Among the clergy present on this occasion we observed the Revs. Mayow, Vincent, Atkinson, Cameron, Dowding, Wilton, Powell, Fort, Pile, Aldwell accompanied by many families of the neighbourhood.'[254]

254 Press report. Devizes Museum Collection.

APPENDIX E

Churchwardens

Bishop's transcripts from the earliest period for which records are available show that the following were churchwardens in the seventeenth century:

1622	John Still
	William Weabe (who signed with his 'mark')
	(Webb also spelt Web)
1623	Thomas Hayward
	William FFord
1626	Philip Dole
	Thomas Boulter
1627	John Still
	Richard Plancke
1628	Gulielmus Webb
	Gulielmus FFoorde[255]
1633	William Web[256]
1634	Thomas FFelps
	Thomas Hayward
1636	William Web
1637	Thomas Hayward
	Thomas FFelps
1654	Steven fflower
	John Still (Both described also as 'overseers of the poore of the parish')

Although a full list of those who have held the office of churchwarden for many of the later years has not been discovered, some names are known:

255 In this year they were given Latin names but are presumably the same as the John Still and William Weabe of 1622. In this year too they were styled 'Aediles'.

256 He is likely to have been the same as the earlier William Weabe, Webb in yet another guise.

1671	Stephen Flower
	Thomas Smith
1705	William Cumlyn
	Brian Hayward
1780	Cumlyn Axford
	William Butcher
1862–78	Samuel Bolter (Rector's)
1878	Richard William Bolter
1880–88	Abraham Bolter
1908	Edmund Bazell
	James Fitch
1942	John Wilfred Nosworthy
1944–55	Dr Newton Dunn
1962–65	D. Oliphant
1961–62	Robert Mouland
1962–72	J. W. Nosworthy
1965–79	Lady Crossley
1973–95	Freddie Child
1980–98	Brigadier Bob Flood
1995	Sir Donald Hawley
1999	Major D. Alcock

APPENDIX F

The Rectors and Incumbents

INCUMBENTS AT LITTLE CHEVERELL

Date	Patron	Name
1297	Alexander Chevrel (Miles)[257]	Williamus de Lavington
1299	Alexander Chevrel (Miles)	Henry de la Forde Rogerus dictus Fraunceys
1329	Nicholaus Pyk, et Joanna uxor ejus[258]	Stephanus de Pendlesford
1339	Nicholaus Pik	Johannes de Brommore
1341	Nicholaus Pik	Simon Perchay
1344	Nicholaus Pik	Thomas de North Cory
1349	Nicholaus Pyk	Johannes Wodefold
1349[259]	Nicholaus Pyk	Robertus Chese
1418	Williamus Dominus de Botreaux	Johannes Perol
1443	Williamus Dominus de Botreaux (Miles)	Georgius Rede pr Williamus Sumner
1465	Margareta Domina Hungerford et Botreaux	Georgius Rede pr Williamus Sumner

257 'Miles', latin for soldier. Therefore a knight owing military service to a higher lord or the King.
258 'And Joanna his wife'.
259 1349 was at the height of the Black Death. It is noteworthy that two appointments were made in Little Cheverell in that year. Perhaps the first incumbent was a victim. It is certain that in 1349 more than a hundred appointments of incumbents in the Diocese were made, compared with an average of ten to fifteen in other years at that period.

1473	Walter Hungerford (Armiger filius et heres Robert Hungerford Dominus de Moleyns et Cheverell Parva)	Walterus Jhoys pr Georgius Rede
1496	Walterus Hungerford (Miles)	Johannes Garnett pr Walter Joys alias Joye
1534	Walterus Hungerford (Miles)	Philippus Stanlake pr Robert Balfront
1554	Maria Regina	Robertus Thomson pr Philippus Stanlake
1577	Walterus Hungerford (Miles)	Henricus Shaw pm Philippi Stanlake
1584	Walterus Hungerford (Miles)	Hugo Gough
1625	Johannes Flower de Melksham ex concess. Franc.Com. Rutland Williamus Pew de Rowdon Wilts et ab illo Johanni Flower	Rogerus Flower pr Hugonis Gough
1660		Edwardus Hort
1667	Edwardus Hungerford (Miles Balnei)[260]	Ricardus Broadhead pm Edwardi Hort
1702	Margaretta Hungerford	Jacobus Meredith pm Ricardi Broadhead
1712	Robertus? Dominus? Lexington	Johannes Gordon pm Jacobi Meredith
1735	Sir Edward des Bouverie of Longford Bart	John Shergold pm John Gordon
1759	Jacob Viscount Folkestone	Joseph Newton pm John Shergold

260 Knight Commander of the Bath (KCB).

1764	William Viscount Folkestone	James Stonhouse pm Joseph Newton
1796	Joseph Earl of Radnor	William Richards[261] pr or pm Sir James Stonehouse
1823	Earl of Radnor	Joseph P. Griffith
1826	Earl of Radnor	John Roles Fishlake
1867	Earl of Radnor	William Powley Nichols
1915	Mr Charles Awdry	Henry P. Margesson
1926	Bishop of Salisbury	Percival Sexty (Canon)
1958	Bishop of Salisbury	Leo V. Porter
1966	Bishop of Salisbury	Patrick Hanna (Canon))
1983	Bishop of Salisbury	Maurice Osborn
1990	Bishop of Salisbury	Hugh Hoskins[262]
1997	Interregnum	
1998	Bishop of Salisbury	Terry Brighton (Priest in Charge)
2002	Bishop of Salisbury	Harold Stephens (Priest in Charge. Rector of Benefice)

261 The Revd William Richards's son John and daughter Sophia were baptised at LC in 1799 and 1800. He was granted 52 acres, 1 rood and 13 perches on East Sandfield and Forehill Common.

262 Hugh Hoskins was the last to hold the freehold of the 'living' as rector. Subsequent appointments have been as 'priest in charge', although the title of rector has continued to be used. Harold Stevens held the title of 'rector' of the combined benefice of West Lavington, Great and Little Cheverell, Market Lavington and Easterton.

INCUMBENTS OF THE CHANTRY OF ST MARY

The incumbents of the Chantry of St Mary were also appointed by the Patron but it was a separate appointment from that of the rector. It may be that a suitable singing voice for chanting the prayers was a special requirement. The appointments were:

Date	Patron	Name
1297	Dominus Alexander Chevrel (Miles)	Ric. De Comyngs?
1299	Alexander Chevrel (Miles)	Rogerus dictus Fraunceys
1308	Alexander de Chevrel (Miles)	Johannes de Cotes
1320	Johannes de Sto. Laudo (Miles)	Henricus de Stodham
1332	Nicholas Pike Dominus[263]	Henricus de Lodyngton
1338	Nicholas Pike, Dominus de Chyverel Parva	Henricus de Lodyngton
1414	Wmus. Dominus de Botreaux (Miles)	Johannes de Yveray, alias Forde vice Wmi. Coke
1416	Wmus. Dominus de Botreaux	Johannes Corbyn
1417	Wmus. Dominus de Botreaux	Stephanus Hull vice Johannes Corbyn
1419	Wmus. Dominus de Botreaux	Rogerus Warde
1423	Wmus. Dominus de Botreaux	Johannes Marnhulle vice Stephanus Hull
1460	Williamus Dominus Botreaux	Johannes Taylour pr Philippi Puttesham

263 Curiously the appointment for this year is recorded as for 'Cantaria in E [Ecclesia] St Nich. De Chyverell Parva' – incidentally confirmation of the Church's dedication to St Nicholas at that time.

APPENDIX G

The Commonplace Book of Thomas Axford

In his commonplace book Thomas Axford,[264] who appears to have been a tough, astute man with a philosophical turn of mind, gives some flavour of life in the village between the 1760s and 1780s. He kept copies in longhand of a number of his letters to members of the Bolter and Wilkins families in Little Cheverell and others elsewhere, which mainly relate to land matters, rents, debts, loads of malt and bills of exchange. He could on occasion be censorious and in one letter to Mr Oram, he writes: 'I am informed that you have had a guest often at your house and have lodg'd her there, which I disapprove of. I think it is not for your credit and may be to my hurt to have such a person in the house. I insist on her not being there.' What was going on is broadly clear but there must be a certain prurient interest in who the lady might have been!

In another letter he writes to 'Mr Cumlyn', of the family with which the Axfords formed close ties, thanking him for the 'kind entertainment of myself and daughters'. In yet another – to Thos. Phipps Esq – Thomas Axford defends himself, writing that he was 'much troubled to think that my Lord[265] have got so ill an opinion of me who have been a Tenant in the family so long'. A copy of another document shows that Thomas Axford the younger was appointed gamekeeper for his land in the Wiltshire manor of Leigh and Ludburn by Granville Wheeler of Otterdean Place in Kent.

Recipes for curing various ailments including gout, fevers and spots are included, as well as directions on the care of the sick and the desiderata of a good 'sick chamber', while a more unusual

264 'Letters, Accounts and Commonplace Book of Thomas Axford 1768–1777.' M/s Box 93, M/ss 1119, Devizes Museum.

265 Mr Phipps was apparently lord of the manor in another parish where Thomas Axford had land holdings.

note is struck by directions for training a horse to lie down on command.

Axford also collected the philosophical expressions of others such as 'Vanity lurks in every heart' and 'Laughter is indeed a very good counterpoise to the spleen'. He obviously knew the then rector, Dr James Stonhouse, well and included the following two poems on his qualities (the second perhaps referring to some abstruse dispute going on in the Close at Bristol) without comment.

To Dr Stonhouse

Whilst dauntless vice pursues its rapid way
And boasts an almost universal sway,
Whilst well-bred priests their easy Virtue bend
To accommodate the failings of a friend,
Too mild, too sympathetically nice
To probe their own or shock their Patron's Vice,
Actively bad or negatively good,
No sin avoided, no Desire withstood.
Whilst these at Folly's Shrine devoutly bend
Shall not religion find one zealous friend?
Yes, Stonhouse: but with life thy care shall cease,
Thou chosen Envoy of the God of Peace.
'Tis not the Stagyrite[266] might praise
The finished meaning in thy polish'd phrase;
Not that thou shunns't the wild enthusiastic Dream
And the dull lifeless Reasoner's cold extreme,
Not thy evangelical pages glow
With all that piety and taste bestow
That thy neglected oratory restore
And Paul at Athens seems to sound once more,
It is not these – the Envoy's self must own –
In these thou stands't unrivalled and alone.
No 'tis thy actions more than sermons teach,
For Stonhouse lives what other only preach.

266 Aristotle.

To Revd Dr Stonehouse

A spruce little Prebend full of his proud station
And the most pious creature in this wicked nation
Declares that the Dean is to the Church untrue,
Nay Stonehouse is either a Pagan or a Jew
O'er the grave of poor Powel for spreading the yew,
But know that dull search for his merit kind Fame,
When thine is forgotten, will Blase his name.

APPENDIX H

Memorandum on the Administration of Little Cheverell School

The School premises are the property of Mrs Charles Awdry (who had acquired it on the death of her husband). They are held by the Managers under agreement between the late Charles Awdry and the late Henry H. Smith[265] dated March 18th 1903 subject to an annual quit rent of one shilling (paid up to Michaelmas 1914) as a Public Elementary School and to be under the Management and control of the Foundation Managers (who shall be members of the Church of England) and two other managers appointed by the Education Authority under the Act of 1902. The Chairman of the Managers is appointed from time to time by the owner of the premises. There is a clause in the agreement directing that religious instruction shall be in accordance with the principles of the Church of England, as by law established as set forth in the Prayer Book and Articles. But the Managers with the approval of the Bishop may appoint on the staff an Assistant Teacher or Monitress who is a Non-Conformist. Expenditure has to be borne by the Managers and the Education Authority and the latter has paid 10/11ths.

267 Builder, of Little Cheverell.

APPENDIX I

The Parish Council

CHAIRMEN SINCE INCEPTION

1975	Mr Freddie Child
1979	Mr Michael Brain
1983	Lady Hawley
1992	Wing Commander Victor King, OBE
1997	Mrs Helena Warnock
2003	Mr George Hockley
2006	Mr Andrew Walker

CLERKS OF THE COUNCIL

Mrs Helena Warnock
Mrs Marie Vine
Mrs Sue Ivey
Mrs Greta Taylor
Mrs Anne Walker
Mr Michael Brain

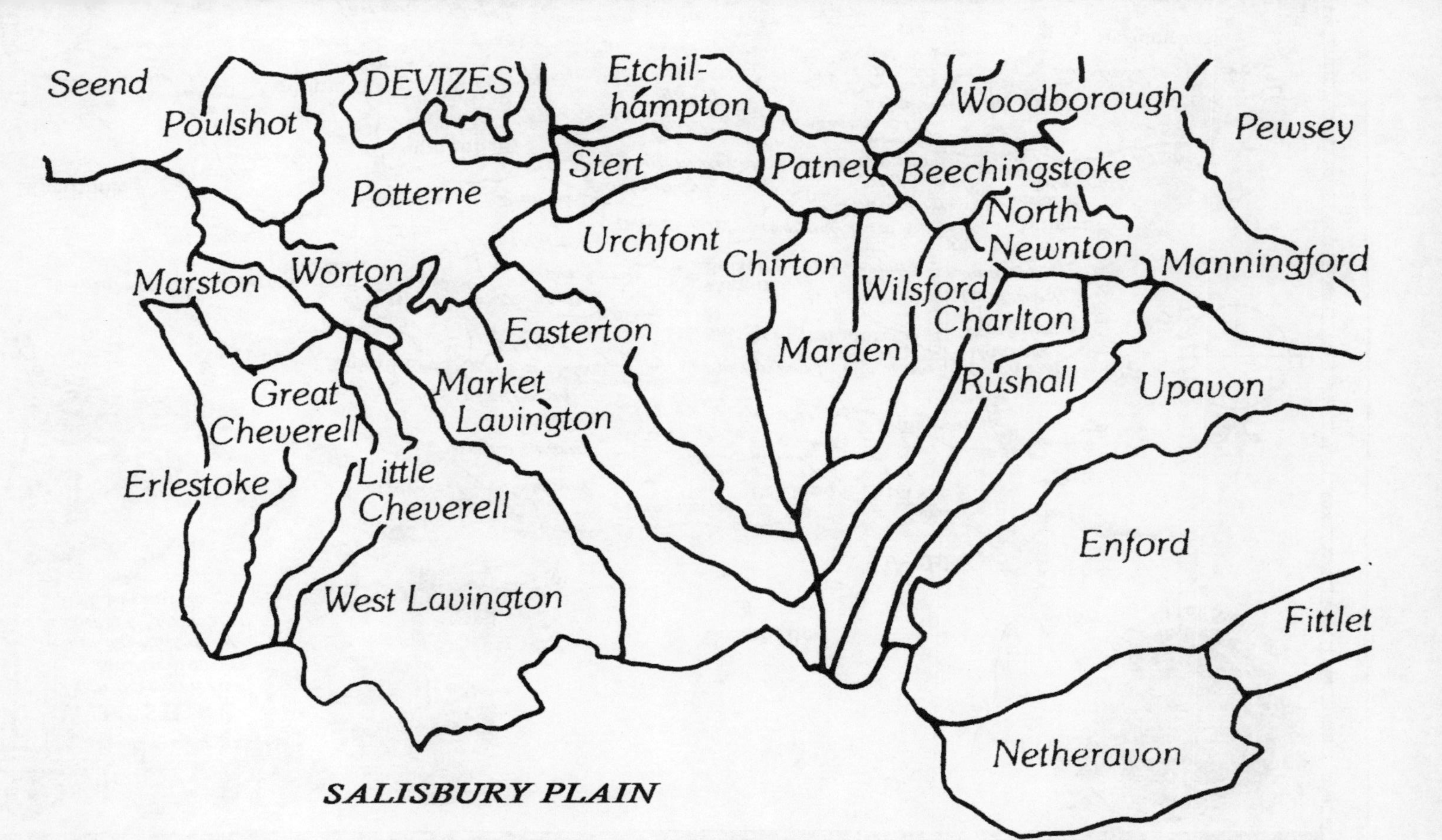

Parishes on the North of Salisbury Plain

For the London Magazine

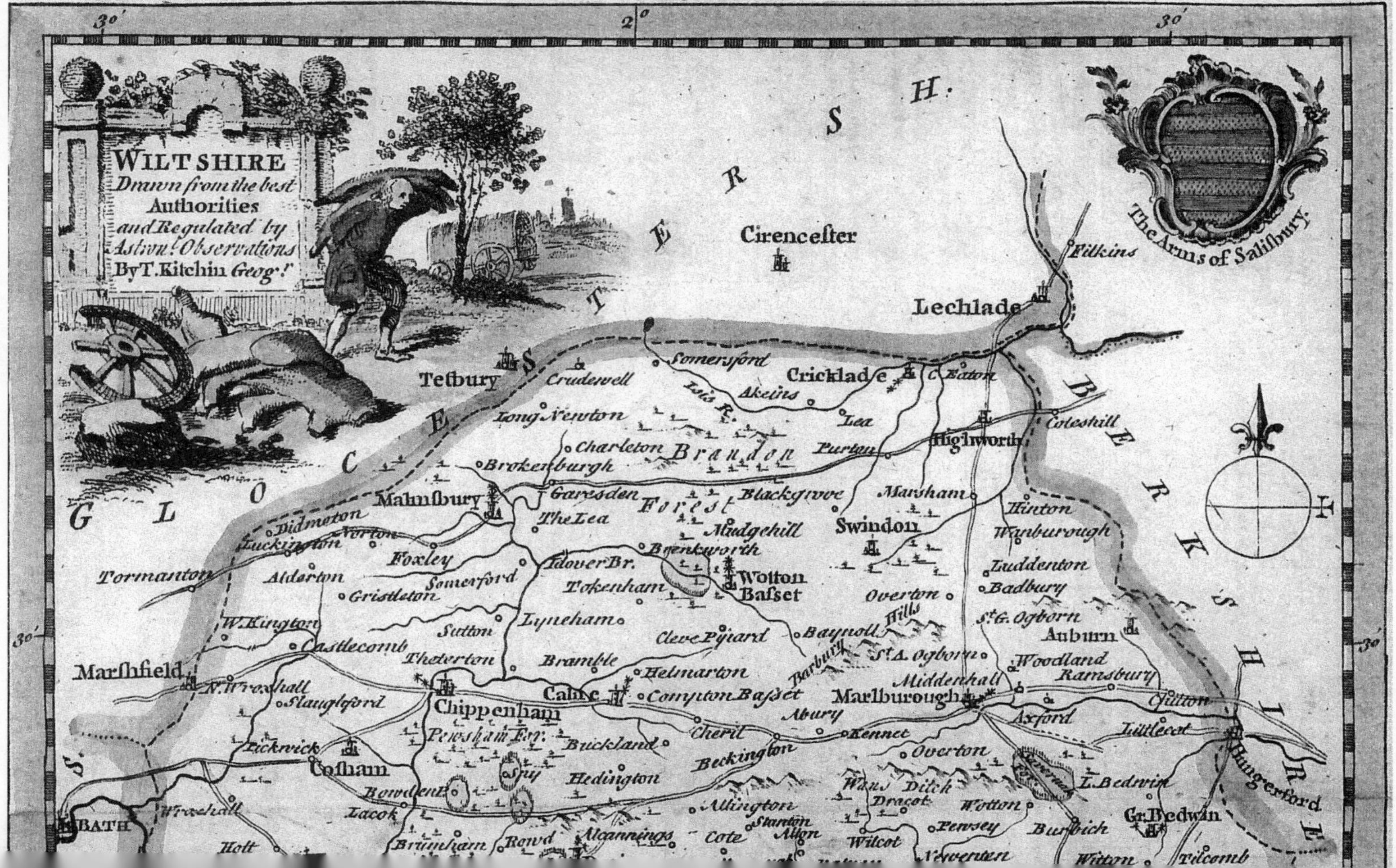
WILTSHIRE
Drawn from the best Authorities and Regulated by Astron. Observations
By T. Kitchin Geog.r
The Arms of Salisbury
GLOCESTERSH.
BERKSHIRE
Cirencester
Lechlade
Tetbury
Malmsbury
Cricklade
Highworth
Swindon
Wotton Basset
Chippenham
Calne
Marlborough
Marshfield
Cosham
Hungerford
BATH

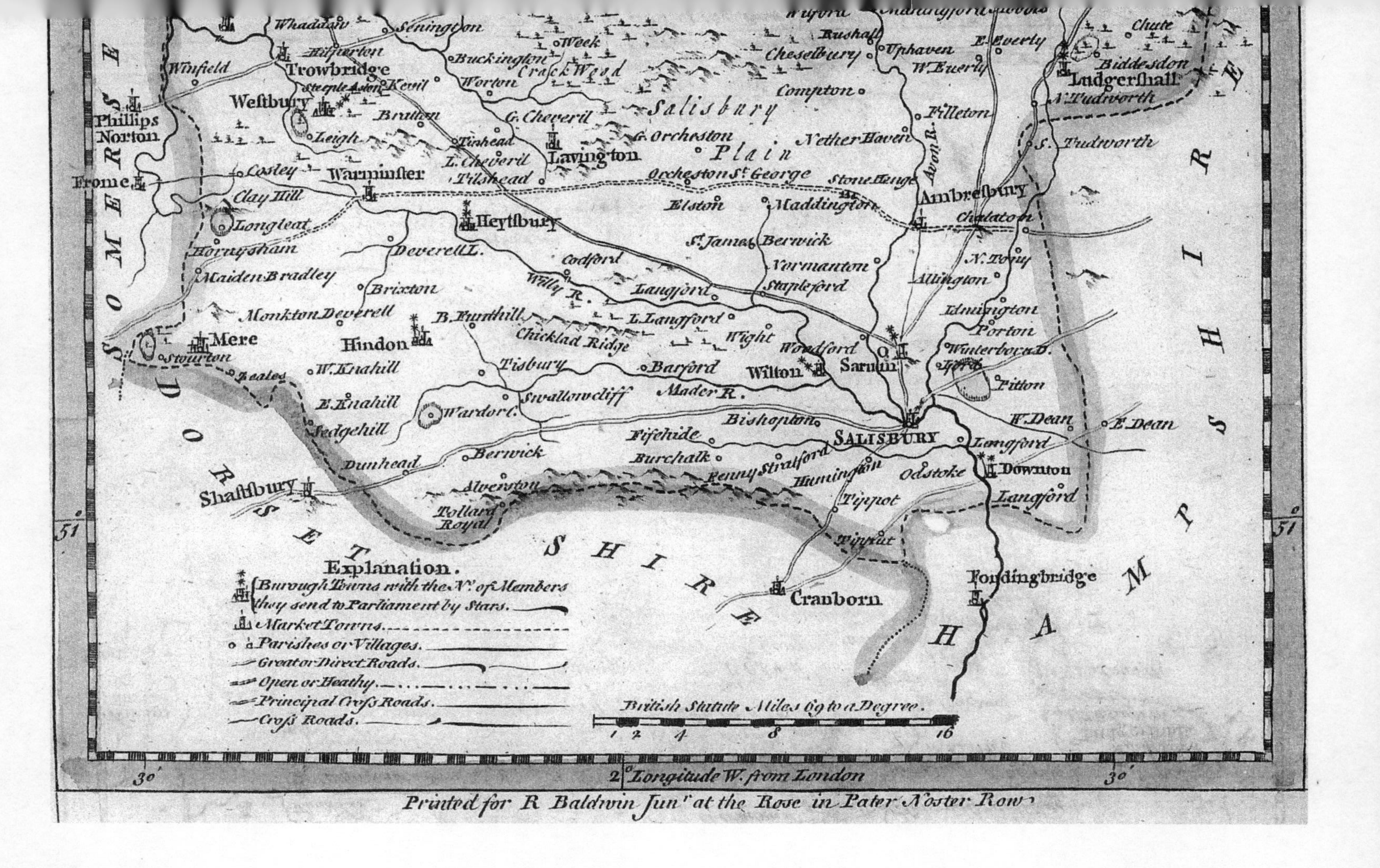
Explanation.
Burough Towns with the No. of Members they send to Parliament by Stars.
Market Towns.
Parishes or Villages.
Great or Direct Roads.
Open or Heathy.
Principal Cross Roads.
Cross Roads.
British Statute Miles 69 to a Degree.
1 2 4 8 16
SOMERSET
DORSETSHIRE
HAMPSHIRE
Salisbury Plain
SALISBURY
Phillips Norton
Frome
Trowbridge
Westbury
Warminster
Heytsbury
Lavington
Hindon
Mere
Shaftsbury
Wilton
Sarum
Ambresbury
Ludgershall
Downton
Fordingbridge
Cranborn
Winfield
Whaddon
Hilperton
Senington
Buckington
Week
Crack Wood
Worton
Steeple Ashton
Kevil
Bratton
Leigh
Tinhead
G. Cheveril
L. Cheveril
Tilshead
Cosley
Clay Hill
Longleat
Horningsham
Maiden Bradley
Deverell L.
Brixton
Monkton Deverell
B. Funthill
Chicklad Ridge
W. Knahill
E. Knahill
Sedgehill
Stourton
Wardort
Tisbury
Swallowcliff
Dunhead
Berwick
Alverston
Tollard Royal
Codford
Willy R.
Langford
L. Langford
Wight
Barford
Mader R.
Woodford
Fifehide
Burchalk
Bishopton
Penny Stratford
Huminghan
Tippot
Wimput
Odstoke
Langford
Downton
E. Dean
W. Dean
Pitton
Winterborn D.
Porton
Idmington
Allington
N. Tony
Chalaton
Maddington
Elston
St. James Berwick
Vormanton
Stapleford
Orcheston St. George
Stone Henge
G. Orcheston
Nether Haven
Compton
Filleton
Avon R.
Rushall
Cheselbury
Upthaven
W. Everly
E. Everly
S. Tudworth
N. Tudworth
Biddesdon
Chute
51
30'
2° Longitude W. from London
Printed for R Baldwin Junr. at the Rose in Pater Noster Row

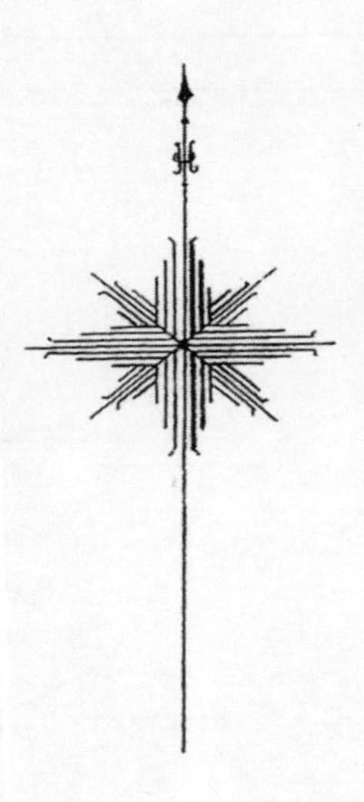

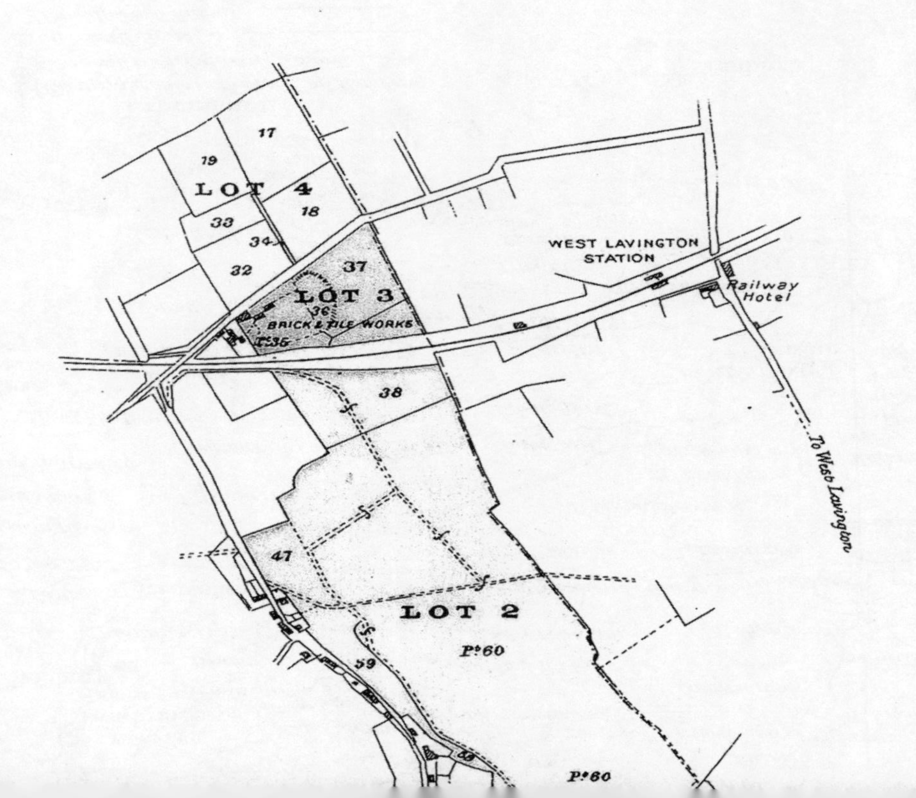

LOT 4
17
19
18
33
34
32
LOT 3
37
36
BRICK & TILE WORKS
35
WEST LAVINGTON
STATION
Railway
Hotel
To West Lavington
38
47
LOT 2
P.t 60
59
P.t 60

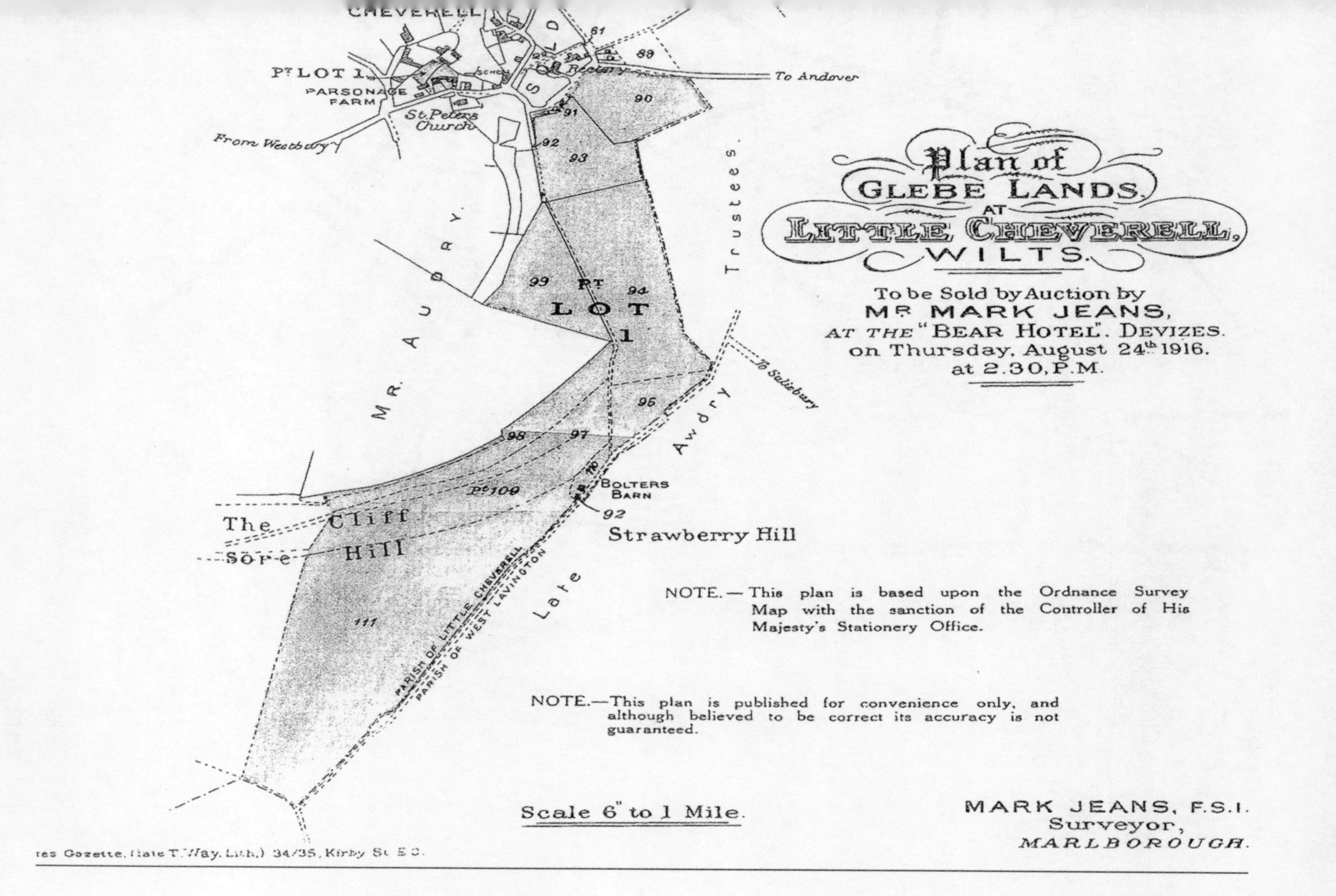

tes Gazette, (late T. Way, Lith.) 34/35, Kirby St. E.C.

Central area of John Edgar's 1722 map of the village (see pp. 22, 46, 56 and 64)

Ashley'd
Orchard
13
Piece
Fore Common
8
20
6
Leases
Pickedfur
Foarding Stile Fur
Fernyland Fur
Made Fur
Becketshedge Fur
Lane End Fur
Furland
Water Fur

Little Chiverell Mannor	
John Axford. Sen	1
John Axford Jun (late Comlins)	2
John Axford Jun	3
Susan Broadhead	4
Thomas Edwards	5
S[r] Edw[d] Des Bouverie (in hand)	6
Mary Minty (in hand)	7
M[r] Gordon (Parsonage)	8
Grace Hampston	9
Ester Hayward. (late Flowers)	10
Ester Hayward (2 Yard lands)	11
Ester Hayward (Haywards)	12
Thomas Hayward	13
Anne Hayward	14

Landholders of numbered areas on preceding map

Little Chiverell Mannor

Index

Sponsors

BARNY AND JUDITH BEDDOW

MICHAEL BRAIN

MICHAEL AND JUDY GAIGER

VINCE AND PAM GAIGER

DONALD AND RUTH HAWLEY

MICHAEL AND LINDA KAVANAGH

MICHAEL MAXWELL

THOMAS MORISON

CATHERINE NOSWORTHY

GRETA TAYLOR

HELENA WARNOCK

ANDREW AND ANNE WALKER